THE TRUE METHOD OF SEARCHING THE SCRIPTURES,

BY

TALBOT FANNING,
PRESIDENT OF FRANKLIN COLLEGE.

CINCINNATI:
AMERICAN CHRISTIAN PUBLICATION SOCIETY.
1854.

TRUE METHOD

OF

SEARCHING THE SCRIPTURES.

SUGGESTIVE THOUGHTS.

In the brief race of life, we all start from the same point. We enter the world unconscious of our origin, of our very existence, and of the objects which surround us; and profoundly ignorant of the dark and dreary future, which spreads out before us. We differ through life in our information, in the part we play in life's drama; and we shall finally differ in the world to come; yet all our differences, to a greater or less extent, depend upon our own exertions. The wisest and best of men become so, by continual labor; while the corrupt and degraded, reap only the reward of their own wicked lives. In our jail and penitentiary reports, we see clearly that, crime most abounds in the hands of ignorance; and while we must admit that, the drunken, profane, and vile of all climes, from their mistakes in the objects of life, bring upon themselves their deepest misery, we are led to ask ourselves the profound question, Why do mortals of earth, sin against God, their Creator and kind Preserver? Solomon has answered the question: "The way of the wicked," said he, "is as darkness; they know not at what they stumble." "Darkness," indeed, "has covered the earth, and gross darkness the people." "The blind lead the blind, and both fall into the ditch together."

No one can walk in the light, who has it not; and if correct moral conduct, spiritual progress, and eternal life, at the end of our earthly journey, depend in the least, upon the quality and amount of our moral light, the study of life should be, to gain true knowledge. It is a singular truth that, men often become quite wise in the affairs of this world, who, nevertheless, remain children in the things that pertain to God; and it is still more strange that, there are large funds of false wisdom, which close the mind and heart to the true fountain, which is able to enlighten every man that comes into the world. The question, "What shall it profit a man if he gain the whole world and lose his own soul?" is not more appropriate than to ask, "What shall it profit us, though we acquire all the knowledge *the world* can furnish, and yet fail to gain 'The true light' which comes from above, and which alone can give assurance of 'That rest which remains for the people of God.'"

PART FIRST.

THE TRUE ORIGIN OF OUR KNOWLEDGE OF GOD, AND OUR DUTIES TO HIM.

INASMUCH as men, for nearly six thousand years, have become virtuous and happy, in the exact ratio of their knowledge of their Creator, and his will concerning them, it is a question of very deep interest to ascertain the proper mode of acquiring this inestimable information. There are three ways, in which it is supposed this knowledge is gained; yet, there can be but one correct source of Divine wisdom. These demand a brief, yet careful examination, at our hands.

FIRST. *It is supposed that Nature affords full information concerning our Father who is in heaven.*

The word Nature is employed; first, to denote the outward world—the heavens with their starry hosts, and the earth, with her ten thousand tongues; and, secondly, it is used to express the supposed world of spontaneous light within—that which is imagined to be natural to the soul.

Wise men, in the different ages of the world, and even christian philosophers, have maintained that, the study of external nature not only affords correct knowledge with regard to the invisible God, but also, furnishes all needful information relative to our duties to our Creator, and to each other. It would be proper to state, in reply, that nature is not a bridge from the visible to the invisible world. The dull matter of the heavens and the earth, with their whole machinery, is insufficient to *suggest* either the existence or perfections of that God who is Spirit. The leap from the visible to the invisible, is not only too great for the philosophy of man, but it is also far above his loftiest imagination. A few plain reasons will justify these conclusions.

When man was first created, his Father and his God, though invisible to us, spoke to him face to face; and it is unreasonable to suppose, that his posterity could entirely lose such information. We, moreover, have heard of no nation acknowledging God, whose information cannot be traced to direct communications, which are as high above nature as God is above man.

Were we to admit that, nature reveals spiritual light, we would be compelled to maintain the sufficiency of this light, to guide us in the path of life.

But facts contradict such a conclusion. They show that those who have been without the Bible, though wise in the things of the world, have known but little of God or his ways, and this little, can be clearly traced to a source different from nature.

When we look into the Scriptures, we find the whole theory contradicted. We are told, "The world by wisdom," philosophy, or the study of nature, "knew not God." "It pleased God, by the foolishness of preaching to save them that believe."

To the enlightened, we rejoice to believe, that, the heavens and the earth, beautifully "declare," impress and confirm, "the glory of God;" but as previously urged, they have no voice to *tell* of the unseen hand which launched them forth.

Those who plead for the inborn light of the soul, to reveal the person and power of our Heavenly Father, must, to be consistent, also maintain the competency of this light, "To lighten every man that comes into the world." Many do so, and further assert, in the style of an old philosopher, that, "This soul of ours, is the divinity within," and is able to guide us into all truth.

Some go even further than this; and tell us, that the soul is either God, or a part of God, and its immortality is its own natural "outgrowth." This theory may seem pretty; but it is not only deceptious, but most dangerous. When we place our highest knowledge in human nature, and declare that eternal happiness, is the legitimate and necessary offspring of the soul, we deny that this wisdom comes through the Bible, and much worse, we virtually say, that redemption is not by Christ, and that he did not really "Bring life and immortality to light in the Gospel." To such, there is no meaning in the death of Christ, and the Bible is worse than a useless book. Indeed, we are sorry to admit, that most, if not all this class of teachers, deny that the Scriptures really *reveal* anything. It is not uncharitable to pronounce them, a sect of deceitful and dangerous speculators.

This pernicious system is now prevailing in Germany, under the head of "Transcendentalism," and wherever it gains footing, God's blessed word is crushed before it.

In France, it speaks out in what is denominated "Social Philosophy." It rejects, everywhere, the authority of the "Written oracles," and calls these pranks before high Heaven, "struggles for liberty;" and even conceals the deadly poison beneath, by throwing over it the mantle of "Charity."

But more need not be said to give the young or old reader, disposed to think, and draw conclusions, a pretty comprehensive idea of the system which claims Nature as a sufficient rule in morality and spirituality.

SECOND. *Many zealous religionists maintain that, all the light from the unseen world, comes in direct revelation of the spirit to each individual.*

Quakers, Shakers, and Mormons, with equal zeal and apparent sincerity, flood the world with their contradictory revelations of the spirit, and to doubt their truth is, in their estimation, to doubt all spiritual religion.

Spiritual Knockers, tell us that, they receive their information from the invisible world, through the ghosts of the departed dead, and a single doubt as to the verity of these new dreams is pronounced illiberality, and uncharitableness; and those who dare do so, are charged with the sin of "opposition to all progress."

The thousands of "seekers of religion" or revelations of forgiveness of sins and acceptance with God, in the divers altars, at the mourner's bench, anxious seat, or in the silent grove, profess to receive direct revelations, and witnesses of the spirit, in impulses, feelings, still small voices, and various other ways, too tedious and revolting to mention. Those who hesitate to admit the truth of these revival revelations, subject themselves to the severe charge of denying all spiritual light and holy influence.

All these, either receive the direct revelations of the spirit, or they do not. They get positive light, or they get nothing. There is no compromise in the matter. Those who profess to receive light in these ways, either experience what they profess, or they are mistaken in their conclusions, and are bewildered in their whole religion.

It might be well to take a bird's-eye view, of the works of these singular systems of Spiritualism.

Is it not a startling truth that, persons inclined to such influence, much prefer their direct revelations, perhaps while asleep, or in answer to their prayers, to the written declarations of the Bible? How could it be otherwise? Who, that could obtain fresh revelations, would be satisfied to labor and toil for the knowledge of God, in the Bible? Indeed, we may justly conclude, as we were compelled to do, in reference to the insufficiency of Nature to reveal the unseen, that when we admit direct and perpetual revelations of the spirit, there is no place or work left on earth for the precious Bible. Thus, direct Spiritualism, banishes the sacred

Scriptures from the world, and leaves nothing in their place.

The effect of these things, is most injurious. Those under their influence, are by no means in a condition to read, hear, or believe the word of God. They are directed by feelings, which they tell us, "make them happy," and they desire nothing beyond. If this were the condition of the ignorant slave, we might entertain strong hopes, that the intelligence of the times, would banish it from our world, but it is seen in high places,—among the learned and influential. It is said, extremes oft meet; and it is somewhat singular that, zealous religionists are not the only persons who advocate the revelations of feelings. Many church members mean nothing more by the direct witness of the spirit, than a hopeful feeling within that God has accepted them in the Beloved. Some who trust to human nature as a guide, profess to walk by a similar inward light of feeling. We are strongly inclined to the opinion that, such persons must follow in part, if not altogether, the inclinations of their own fleshy desires and fickle passions. It is well known that, the celebrated infidels, Voltaire and Helvetius, advocated the unlimited gratification of their fleshy appetites. The famous scoffer Rousseau, who, according to his own printed reports, was a thief, a falsifier, and a profligate, had recourse to *feeling* as his standard of morality.

"I have only to consult myself," said he, "concerning what I do. All I feel to be right, is right; what I feel to be wrong, is wrong. All the morality of our actions lies in the judgment we ourselves form of them. The tendency of the philosophy, learning and religion of the age, is to make an infallible spiritual standard of each one's passions, desires and feelings. The charitable doctrine in most of the churches is, what each thinks and feels in his own conscience to be right, is right to him."

Men, of course, who preach this, must be popular; such flattery of the flesh, could but delight the sensual. These men gravely pronounce opposition to these sentiments, "dogmatism, popery, and tyranny;" and boldly deny that, there is a written standard in religion. The Apostle Peter very strikingly describes them thus:

"There are wells without water, clouds that are carried with the tempest; to whom the mist of darkness is reserved forever. For when they speak great swelling words of vanity, they allure through the lusts of the flesh, through much wantonness, those that were clean escaped from them who live in error. While they promise them liberty, they themselves are the servants of corruption."

But the reader need not be further detained, in examination of false revelations, and systems which have been of no service to the world.

THIRD. *The best of men, since the establishment of the christian religion, have maintained that, the Bible fairly translated into the various languages of earth, is the only safe guide in all spiritual investigations.*

On this part of the subject, it will be in place to state clearly, the Romanish and Protestant positions.

The Roman Catholic Church, while she has advocated the inspiration of the Holy Scriptures, has never admitted that, the Bible is a rule of life, adapted to the people. Indeed, she has always maintained that, the *naked* Scriptures should not be read by the people.

In this, she is consistent; for she thinks the Bible has divers and diverse meanings, which the common people cannot understand. Hence the struggle in the United States, to keep the Bible out of schools, which Romish children attend.

The Romish position is, that the Scriptures must be *interpreted* by the doctors of the church; and these interpretations, with the decrees of the authoritative councils and the *traditions* of the fathers, constitute the only infallible rule in the church.

Protestants deny the decrees of the Romish Church, and the traditions; but they suppose the Scriptures are not, *in form,* a rule of life. The true Protestant position is, that it remains for each sect, to give authoritative interpretations of the Bible, to suit the various ages and circumstances of the people, and yet they say, their members have the right of private judgment, or individual interpretations; but they are scrupulously careful that, these private interpretations of the Bible, agree with the higher interpretations of the respective churches. We shall next examine, what we most sacredly regard, as the Christian position.

We believe and teach that, the Heavenly Father gave a perfect code of laws to the Jews, which were adapted to the understanding of the people; and that every effort to interpret them, in a sense which would imply that, they could be improved by man, was a gross departure from authority. Hence the Savior charged the Jews with the sin of rejecting the commandments of God, by their traditions.

We believe and teach that, the New Testament is a "*perfect law of liberty,*" and that it is in *matter and form*, sufficient to make all "wise unto salvation" who will follow its teachings.

The most wonderful feature in the New Testament, is its perfect adaptation to Christians in all time and in all circumstances of life. The man of deep learning may employ all his days in reading profitably the sacred oracles; and yet, so simple are parts of this "Last will and testament" of our Lord that, in the language of the prophet, "Though fools, they shall not err therein."

Each article of faith or item of belief is forcibly, and yet more handsomely expressed in the Bible, than in any other book on earth. Each duty to God, is fully revealed and forcibly written, and all church obligations and injunctions to the world, are clearly set forth.

Thus, we are fully prepared to answer the question, as to the origin of the knowledge of God and our information in reference to the invisible world.

The Bible is, undoubtedly, the only medium of communication between mortals of earth, and God their Maker. This proposition is sustained by the fact that, in no country or age has man's spiritual acquisitions transcended the information furnished in the Bible. We are sorry to know that, even in this favored land, it is contended that, the Bible without an additional inspiration, is not sufficient for spiritual light. Still they tell us, in the next breath, that "The heathen are perishing for lack of the knowledge which the Bible affords." Thus it seems, according to these statements, that, while the Scriptures, to be efficacious at home, must be accompanied by other and higher revelations of the spirit, in less favored lands, and such as have no Bibles, there is no spiritual light. Man is often inconsistent in his ways. Take from us the precious oracles of God, and the sun of the moral world will be blotted out, and man, with all his boasted attainments, will, in a few generations, fall into ignorance and a life of barbarism. *Good* and *evil*, where the Bible is not, are words without meaning.

PART SECOND.

RULES FOR STUDYING THE BIBLE.

RULE I. *We must be satisfied, before we can read the Scriptures understandingly, or profitably, that our kind Father intended them for his erring creatures of earth.*

THEY are not addressed to angels, demons, infants, or idiots; but to lost sinners who need a Savior. If the precious oracles had been addressed to a chosen few called preachers, or expounders, the people would be dependent upon mortal aid and doubtful expositions for light; but we should thank God, that this rich source and pure fountain of truth, like rippling streams and cooling brooks to the thirsty, flows even to us, most unworthy creatures. If we fail learning the truth as it is in Christ Jesus, great will be our ignorance, and sad our misfortunes. Said the blessed Savior, "My words shall judge you in the last day." We should not forget that God gave his word to man in his fallen and condemned state, and that it was his design to adapt it to all his spiritual wants. In the clearness of this pure light, the primitive Christians sincerely rejoiced, and triumphed amid persecutions and the severest trials. The timid were made strong, even in prison, and the consuming flames.

In trusting frail man's opinions, there is always doubt; but the poor wanderer of earth, who regards the Bible as "The light to his feet and lamp to his path," can say, "I know if this earthly house of my tabernacle were dissolved, I have a building of God, a house not made with hands, eternal in the Heavens."

This point admitted, we shall be encouraged to believe that, the Bible is not a sealed book—that it is what it purports to be—a volume of revelations from Heaven. True, there are things, "hard to be understood, which they that are unlearned and unstable, wrest to their own destruction," yet the great and cardinal features of the Bible are so plain and so impressive, that "he that runs may read." Children need not err in the practices of the Scriptures. No one should blind his eyes to the meaning of sin, and its deplorable consequences. "All unrighteousness is sin;" and while we look into the Bible as a mirror, that reflects perfectly our moral features, we may be changed into the image of our God, "From glory to glory, even as by the Spirit of the Lord."

If parents, in sending their children to school, should be so unfortunate as to select teachers who would impress the young mind with the idea that, their books were incomprehensible—too difficult to be mastered,—discouragement would press heavily upon their young and timid hearts, and the confidence so essential to success, would be taken from them. No threats or stripes can enable them to surmount the obstruction. The child is at least half educated, when it becomes fully inspired with the idea, enforced by Napoleon upon a young man who hesitated at his task, by telling him that, "A youth should regard nothing as impossible."

When, therefore, we open the divine volume, we should not only consider it as God's book to the lost, but sufficiently plain for all to read with marked advantage. With such encouragements we may gather rich jewels from every page.

Rule II. *In reading the Bible, the study of words is not to be disregarded.*

In reading a plain history, we often, by neglecting the meaning of a few simple words, soon find ourselves bewildered and discouraged—the book becomes tiresome, and we lay it aside, either in disgust, or with the saddening thought that, we are not competent to grasp its meaning. Too often, we read in such haste that, we can make nothing our own. Far better would it be, to read a passage, or chapter, two or three, or even a dozen times, than to glide over it, without properly digesting the matter contained in it. The great and learned men of the world agree that, each word has one, and but one, literal meaning. No word, in its introduction, was ever used figuratively; but was intended to express a thought; and hence, words are said, rightly, to be signs of ideas. If the word is employed to express an action, the action is one, and never two. Thus *run*, always carries with it a single idea, whether the object is to express the running of a man; the running of a horse; the running of a steamboat, or railroad-car. If the writer intends by a word, to denote an object, we must bear in mind, if the word is appropriate, it gives the full image of the object to the mind, or it gives nothing. Thus, the word *boat*, invariably presents to the mind a water craft, of some kind, and nothing else. It is proper to say that, words are frequently employed out of their literal use, and then, they are said to be metaphorical.

But we must not infer that, a figurative use of the word gives a new and original meaning. True, the learned *Ernesti* tells us that, "A metaphorical meaning sometimes, by use, becomes the literal signification of the word." Use has also changed its relations to other words. We should not forget to impress the reader with the thought expressed by Archbishop Whately that, "Metaphysical meanings, as long as words retain their original meaning, must conform to their literal signification."

Although words in the same book, and on the same page, are applied differently, they still center in a single *root* meaning. In examining a word, therefore, we should endeavor in the first place, to get "its heart, from which, as from a fruitful seed, all the others unfold themselves." We will introduce to the reader's attention, the authority of the very learned and accurate thinker, R. C. French, Professor of Divinity in King's College, London. He says, "A word has originally but one meaning, and that all others, however widely they may diverge from one another, and seem to recede from this one, may yet be affiliated upon it, may be brought back to the one center meaning, which grasps and knits them altogether; just as the races of men; black, white and red, despite of their present diversion and dispersion, have a central point of unity in their first parents. Here is the word 'post;' how various are the senses in which it is employed; 'post-office,' 'post-haste,' a 'post' standing in the ground, a military 'post,' an official 'post,' to 'post' a ledger.

Might not one, at first, presume it impossible to bring all these uses of '*post*' to a common center? Yet, indeed, when once on the right track nothing is easier; 'post' is the Latin '*positus*,' that which is *placed;* the piece of timber is 'placed' in the ground, and so a 'post;' a military station is a 'post,' for a man is 'placed' in it, and must not quit it without orders; to travel 'post,' is to have certain relays of horses 'placed' at intervals, so that no delay on the road may occur; the 'post'-office, is that which avails itself of this mode of communication; to 'post' a ledger, is to 'place' or register its several items." Hundreds of similar examples might be given, but the result would be the same.

In reading the Bible, suppose the first word that meets the eye, is 'faith.' If we cannot find a satisfactory meaning in the dictionary, we might refer the sense to the decision of the Scriptures. In opening at the 11th chapter of Hebrews and first verse, we are informed that, "Faith is the substance, (confidence) of things hoped for, and evidence of things not seen." This is satisfactory without comment or explanation; and whenever we find the word in the Bible, we may rest assured, the idea is that of confidence in the truth of what is written. Thus, it is our rejoicing confidence that, Christ died for our sins; that he rose from the dead for our justification; and that if we follow him, through evil, as well as good report, our heartfelt conviction is that, we shall reign with him in heaven.

In the word 'church,' we have the simple idea of an assemblage of persons, without regard to the business for which they may be convened; but when we see the phrase, "Church of Christ," we have the idea of a company of Christ's disciples—a body of the Saints.

What a vast amount of evil might be averted, if religious teachers and students of the Bible, would apply this rule to many words in reference to which the controversies are so exciting; as the word 'repent,' and the word 'baptize.' Each has a definite meaning and may be easily learned. If, for instance, '*baptize*' is a word of any language, we know it has one meaning and but one. Whatever it might be, it should be written in the Bible, and this, and this alone, would put an end to all strife on this long vexed question. Indeed, most, if not all religious controversies might be easily settled in this manner. But time and space fail us to say half that might be useful to the young student of the Bible upon this very important rule.

Rule III. *We should read, not to prove a system, but to learn the truth.*

Most persons are brought up with unyielding prejudices in favor of a particular denomination or system of religion. Denominational prejudices seldom, if ever, fail to warp the judgment and bias the conclusions. When the Bible is read as a *text* or *proof*-book, it seems impossible to learn the truth as it is set forth. Suppose we admit, in obedience to the ordinary custom of preaching from texts, that there is matter in each verse for a sermon, and in many instances, in each clause of a verse in the Bible, and that this is the true mode of getting at the sense of the Scriptures, in what time, could a diligent learner, become familiar with the Bible? If we were all to live to the age of Methuselah, we would be but beginners in the science of religion. But when we take into consideration the fearful truth that, at least half of these text sermons are preached as far *from* the text as Heaven is from earth, we begin to doubt whether we would receive more error than truth in such a procedure. A correct history of such preaching would have the subject of spiritual improvement in fearful doubt, to say the least.

When the Bible is read as a text-book, of course, it is presumed there is no connection in the divine oracles, and that the different parts contribute but little, if any, to a satisfactory solution of the whole record. In this view, the Bible is a book of proverbs and disjointed sentences and clauses, each of which has to be studied independently of all the rest. On this plan, anything, everything may be proved with equal ease. Have not the most contradictory systems been established by this license with the word of God? Each system is presumed to be *independent* of the Bible, and to have an existence without it. In reading the various creeds, few, if any, of the articles, are in the words and forms of the Scriptures; but their framers tell us that, they agree with the Bible, and are the very essence of God's word. It is an alarming error to conclude that, there are Bible ideas, which cannot be expressed in the words of the Bible. When we prefer other forms of speech, it is a tacit admission that, we are best pleased with things which are not sacred; and, indeed, that we are not dependent for our religious information upon the plain teachings of the Scriptures. As intimated, all human systems are made on this plan.

Were it our object to prove the truth of Romanism, granting us this liberty, we should read the Bible with the idea that, it was our business, to find all the Catholic passages in the Scriptures. In the first place, other passages could have but little, if any, effect upon our minds. It is doubtful, whether, adopting this mode of investigation, we could receive the proper impression of *the meaning of one* verse in a thousand. But in the prosecution of our labor, we would begin to read with our articles in our mind and heart; and, perhaps, in Genesis, Exodus, or some one of the five books of Moses, we might, perhaps, find a single verse or clause, in unison with our creed;—this passage, we would mark as suitable; and to conform to general custom, we would *extract* it from its connection, and append it as proof to one of our cherished articles. Thus, we might proceed through both the Old and New Testament, cutting, carving, and splitting the sentences of the Bible, to get proofs for our systems. In this manner, we might demonstrate, at least to our satisfaction, that the good Peter was not only *a* rock, but by selecting an article from one part, and a noun from another, possibly, we might prove that he was *the* rock, on which Christ built His church; and with a slight effort of imagination, we might make this same modest Peter the head of the church and the first Roman pontiff.

But could we not quite as easily establish Calvinism or Armenianism, in this same manner? Who would find it an arduous task to prove universal salvation without regard to conduct or character, with such liberty? Did we design to prove Universalism, we would select such passages as, "God sent not his son into the world to condemn the world; but that the world through Him might be saved," (Jno. iii, 17); "God is the Savior of all men," (1 Tim. iv, 10), etc. Where is the evil? Is it not too much to assert that, the very words of the Bible, convey a false idea when they are detached from their connection. In keeping with the declaration that, "God sent not his son to condemn the world," it is said by our Lord, "He that believeth not, is condemned already, because he had not believed in the name of the only begotten son of God," (Jno. iii, 18); and while Paul says: "God is the Savior (preserver) of all men," in the very next words, he informs us that, He is "specially" a Savior "of those that believe."

Might we not quite as adroitly prove, by this mode, that, there is no God, or that, there are many Gods — as many as the Greeks, Romans, and Egyptians worshiped? We find the words in the Bible, "there is no God,"—this is enough to show the point;—but the whole passage asserts that, "The fool has said in his heart, there is no God." Ps. xiv, 1. The Apostle tells us, "There be that are called Gods, whether in Heaven or on earth, (as there be gods many, and lords many) but to us there is but one God, the Father," (1 Cor. viii, 5, 6). But does not the reader perceive that, with such an object in view, in reading the Scriptures, there is neither probability or possibility of aiming at the truth?

We may gravely ask, when we observe so many contradictions in the various denominations, how shall we read the Bible to profit? There is no doubt our Heavenly Father intended that his word should make all proper moral impressions on the mind; and necessarily, the first object to attain is, to remove every obstruction between the heart and the Divine volume. We should endeavor, in reading, to stand erect before God, and if possible, forget all prejudice, and we are not sure but it would be well, to forget all we believe of a religious character. Having thus brushed the clouds out of our way, we should say with the good Samuel, "Speak Lord, for thy servant heareth."

We recollect a good illustration of the rule, with an excellent preacher and his faithful wife. They had long been in clouds and darkness in relation to many things in the Bible. The fact is, they had received from their early teachers things that were not true, yet from long habit, they loved them; but in reading they could not get them and the Bible in unison. The struggle was intense; but as the preacher's heart finally yielded to the Spirit's teaching, instead of the teaching of men, he said to his wife, "Let us open the book, and hear God speak, while we will be content to listen to what he says." The triumph was complete —traditions were abandoned, God spoke to the heart through his word—both grew

"Strong in the Lord and in the power of his might." This humble man told us, years afterward, that, he never afterward entertained a doubt as to his position in religion. Indeed, there is no occasion to doubt, if we believe through the truth "as it is written."

Hence, in reading Genesis i, 1, "In the beginning God created the Heaven and the earth," we should not ask, What does this prove? but, What does it teach? Moses had no geological theory to prove, and he intended, simply, to state that, "First of all, God made the Heaven and the earth"—God is the Author of all. When the Savior said, "Go teach the nations, baptizing them into the name of the Father, Son and Holy Spirit," the only question should be, What does Christ say? If we know his will, happy will we be, if we do it. Proceeding to read in this mannner, we cannot see how any one can fail to learn the truth in its simplicity and power.

Rule IV. *We should read the Bible with the idea that, God is his own interpreter, and he has made it plain.*

Unfortunately for the world, the Romish doctors, at an early period in the history of the church, authoritatively established the dogma that, the Bible could be of no service without a church interpretation. From that sad hour, the precious oracles have been vailed. While Protestants deny the authority of the Romish priests, to interpret for the world, they maintain the right of "private judgment," in the sense that, each individual is authorized to make a creed to suit himself; so it does not contradict the creed of the respective party. If the world understood, by private judgment, the right of every one to read, understand and believe the Scriptures as they are written, not only would all good men concur, but such a rule, faithfully carried out, would rid the world of much idle speculation. Our observation of those who advocate, what they are pleased to call, "liberty of conscience," under the head of "private judgment," leads us to the conclusion that, their pretended right to "think for themselves," not only gives each one the liberty to construct and maintain, the wildest views; but as a class, they are generally as exclusive and overbearing, as the Pope himself. While the Romanists advocate one authoritative system of interpretations, the "private judgment" of the age emboldens the millions to make an infallible rule of their whims, caprices and fleshly passions, under the imposing head of "*freedom*." The fact is, men are entitled to no authoritative opinions, in religion; and if they even honestly miss the truth, as our mother Eve did, in eating the forbidden fruit, it is at their own peril. God says, (Isai. lv, 8, 9), "My thoughts are not as your thoughts, neither are your ways as my ways. For as the Heavens are higher than the earth, so are my ways higher than your ways, and my thoughts than your thoughts." Men speak and write upon this subject, as if the Bible were not a revelation. It should be remembered that, a revelation is a development of things not previously known, and, if we agree that, God made the revelations attributed to him, it would be an extremely strange conclusion for us to suppose, they are not as plain as their Author intended they should be; or that they are not completely adapted to those for whom they were intended, and perfectly satisfactory.

But not to be tedious, the Bible, is really and, to all intents and purposes, a book of explanations and interpretations of God's mind to the world. When, therefore, we say it is a revelation, explanation and interpretation of our Heavenly Father's will, it would be highly incongruous, to maintain, this revelation, had yet to be revealed, or that these explanations or interpretations, still demanded explanations and interpretations, in the sense, at least, in which these words are used in modern time. It must be offensive to the Majesty of Heaven and earth, to assert, His interpretations and revelations, still require expositions to adapt them to man. If God required an interpreter, mortals should not be selected for the purpose. Jesus Christ came, "To make known," reveal, "his Father to the world;" and his work is so perfect that, every effort to make it plainer, only "darkens counsel with words without meaning."

All the sacred records contradict the

supposition that, an interpreter is needed. Words, as we have learned, are the signs of ideas, and when we admit that, Jehovah employed the words and phrases with which his creatures were familiar, it is not reasonable to suppose, that everything is not as plain, as God himself could make it.

A few examples from the Scriptures will, we think, settle this apparently difficult question.

Our Savior said, "He that believeth on me, as the Scripture hath said, out of his belly shall flow rivers of living water," (Jno. vii, 38). Notice, gentle reader, we are to believe as the Scriptures have said. How is this done, but in the very words of the Scriptures? In the ever-memorable prayer of our Lord, the subject is brought vividly to view thus, "Neither pray I for these alone, but for them also who shall believe on me through their word; that they all may be one, as thou, Father, art in me, and I in thee, (Jno. xvii, 20). It is not difficult to see, that correct belief in Jesus Christ, is through the word of the Apostles. They spoke as the Spirit gave them words, or "utterance," and the words believed put the hearers in possession of the faith, the end of which, is the salvation of the soul.

In the great commission, the apostles are commanded to, "Preach the Gospel." Mind, they are not authorized to expound, explain or interpret the Gospel, but simply to preach it. They had no right to express the slightest opinion concerning it, under the false show of freedom—liberty of conscience—and had they done so, they would have forfeited all respect as credible witnesses and ministers of the *word*.

Why was such a mission given? Did not our Lord know that the Gospel was, and is, completely adapted to all for whom it is intended? The simple, plain, and naked truth, when fairly translated, is in the only form the belief of which will constitute Christian faith. The belief of expositions, interpretations and opinions of the word, is not the faith that brings to the soul peace and full satisfaction.

In Paul's last letter to his beloved Timothy, he says: "I charge thee, therefore, before God, and the Lord Jesus Christ, who shall judge the quick and the dead, at his appearing and his kingdom; Preach the word," (2 Tim. iv, 1, 2). Can the reader farther doubt that a hearty belief of the very words of the Bible, is the only true faith?

How pleasant it is to reflect that, when we read or hear the word of God, we are in the closest converse with our Father in Heaven,—with our blessed Savior Jesus Christ, and with the God-Spirit, our advocate of the Christian institution! When we believe and obey these words, we believe and obey God, and enjoy all correct assurances of acceptance with our Creator. The many exceedingly great and precious promises of the Bible, afford to the pious heart a hope, which "Is an anchor to the soul, both sure and steadfast, and which entereth into the veil, whither the forerunner has entered for us." Are we told that, on this plan, we have no use for preachers to be called of God, to make known the glad tidings? True, if we know the truth already, it cannot be made known to us a second time, and we are willing to admit that, we have no men called now, as were the ambassadors of our Lord. When they were commissioned, the New Testament was not written, and its contents were not known. These preachers had the treasures of the Gospel in "earthen vessels"—they were the sacred reservoirs of the fountain of wisdom, into which the angels in vain, desired to look. They "brought glad-tidings of good things," which no preacher now "brings." Nevertheless, God makes it the duty of "faithful men" in this age, as he has done since the Gospel was first published, to announce the things that are written for the salvation of the ruined sons and daughters of earth. Consequently, all Christians are called to their respective duties in proportion to the "ability" of each, and happy shall he or she be, who does the will of the Father.

Rule V. *The different portions of the Scriptures, should be read with direct reference to their legitimate connections.*

If a passage should appear difficult at the first reading, we should carefully examine all parallel passages; and we would soon learn that, the different parts, furnish perfect commentaries. In thus "comparing spiritual things with spiritual," we could scarcely fail to learn the true intent and purpose of the various writers.

Should we, for instance, desire to study the subject of Faith, we would act wisely in comparing a number of connections and passages on this subject. In thus comparing the Scriptures, we would learn, 1st, that, "Faith is the substance of things hoped for, and the evidence of things not seen," (Heb. xi, 1); 2dly, that "Faith comes by hearing, and hearing by the word of God," (Ro. x, 17); 3dly, that, "With the heart man believeth unto righteousness, and with the mouth confession is made unto salvation," (Ro. x, 10); 4thly, that, "He that believeth on the Son hath everlasting life," (Jno. iii, 36); and in the 5th, and last place, that, "Whosoever believeth on him (the Son) shall not be ashamed." Ro. ix, 33. In the same manner, we may examine most scriptural subjects with equal satisfaction.

Ofttimes, by looking at a single passage without regarding the connection, we are liable to be deceived, and thrown into dangerous errors. Especially, should we look narrowly at the context of everything that strikes us as being difficult; and, we should not hasten to conclusions, before we have finished the connection. For illustration, the apostle Paul introduces an argument in the first part of the epistle to the Hebrews, which he does not close, till he reaches the tenth chapter. Other examples might be adduced, but we deem them unnecessary.

RULE VI. *In reading, attention should be given to the character of the persons addressed.*

Parts of the Bible were written exclusively for the Jews, and can strictly be applied to no other people; other parts, are intended for the world, or such as profess no religion; and again, we have many books which were designed for churches or individual Christians alone. The repeated failures, in this particular, produce the greatest confusion of society, of which mention is made in the Scriptures. The reader will find a good illustration in the wise judgment of the Lord, in confounding the tongues in the building of the tower of Babel. The condition of affairs, when the languages were confounded, leads us immediately to conclude that, the workmen were prevented from proceeding in the enterprise, from incapacity to express the name of the work intended, and the character of the assistants necessary to carry it forward. Thus the superintendent, who desired "more brick," would cry out for mortar; another, who desired stones, would call for grass; and still another, who wanted more timber, would vociferate, water, water! The consequence was, the tower could go no higher; but stood as an eternal monument of man's folly and utter incapacity to construct any edifice resembling the works of the Father. Not so in building the ark. Noah worked under divine directions, and every part proceeded in its proper order to completion. Not thus, in the erection of the Temple by Solomon. Rules were given for the preparation of all the materials, and when they were brought together, "there was not the sound of a hammer or any iron instrument," in rearing that most splendid edifice of earth. "God was in it."

Neglect of this rule, is the most fruitful source of the disputes and contradictions of the various denominations in our own times. A few illustrations will be of service.

In the days of King Solomon, it was "Better to go to the house of mourning, than to the house of feasting," and hence the people of the Lord took much interest in sympathizing with their afflicted brethren. The Apostle exhorts to "weep (mourn) with them that weep, and rejoice with them that rejoice." Christians are always benefited by mingling their sorrows and tears with those of the distressed. They feel that, "Sorrow is better than laughter," and by the "sadness of the countenance, the heart is made better." But when the Christian duty, and Christian privilege of mourning, is applied to the world, with the promise that by mourning for sins, they shall be forgiven, the whole subject is thrown into sad confusion. It places the sinner in extreme doubt, whether Christ has any positive appointment for remission to aliens, and thus, he is led into the most extravagant experiments to gain the power of God. This confusion arises from misapplying the declaration of the Savior to his disciples, on the Mount, when they were separate from the multitude, "Blessed are they that mourn; for they shall be comforted." Mat. v, 4. That it was addressed to the disciples alone, is obvious, from the parallel passage in Luke. "And he lifted up his eyes on his disciples, and said, Blessed be ye poor; for yours is the kingdom of God. Blessed are ye that hunger now; for ye shall be filled. Blessed are ye that *weep* (mourn) now; for ye shall laugh. Blessed are ye when men shall hate you, and when they shall separate you from their company, and shall reproach you, and cast out your names as evil for the Son of man's sake. Rejoice ye in that day and leap for joy; for behold, your reward is great in Heaven." Luke vi, 20–22. When the sinner is put to struggling and mourning for something, he knows not what; but with the faint hope that, light will burst upon the soul, when, perhaps, he is least anticipating it, his condition is truly pitiable. There is in the practice a most dangerous deception. The horrors of the damned are portrayed in the darkest colors, and his own character is presented as the worst in existence, for the purpose of thrusting him, as nearly as possible, into the regions of "the awful gulf;" and it is well understood that, the lower the miserable victim can be sunk, the more speedily will exhausted nature react. So soon as the worst of this fearful storm of feeling has past, the patient, of course, feels that, his bitter tears have washed away a part at least, if not all his load of anguish; and this effort of overburdened nature to be free, is whispered into the deceived heart, as religion, and a clear receipt of remission. This trick of the age, arises from applying to penitents Scriptures which were never designed for them. Another example may be drawn from the address of Paul to Christians, "Let a man examine himself, and so let him eat of that bread and drink of that cup." 1 Cor. xi, 28. It will not be forgotten that, "Many of the Corinthians hearing, believed, and were baptized." Acts xviii, 8. But this preparatory examination, which was enjoined exclusively on such as had believed with all the heart unto righteousness, renounced their sins, and been baptized into Christ; when applied to saints and sinners indiscriminately, with the exhortation to examine themselves, and if they "feel worthy to partake of the Lord's Supper," is well calculated to scandalize this most solemn feast of the church of God. A third and last example, may be drawn from the practice of the different denominations in directing the last in the way of salvation.

To the jailer, Paul said: "Believe on the Lord Jesus Christ, and thou shalt be saved and thy house," (Acts xvi, 31); to other inquiries, an inspired apostle said: "Repent, and be baptized every one of you, in the name of Jesus Christ, for the remission of sins, and you shall receive the gift of the Holy Spirit," (Acts ii, 38); but again, a sinner is told to "Arise and be baptized, and wash away his sins, calling on the name of the Lord." Acts xxii, 16. Are not these Scriptures quoted, by the most popular preachers, for the purpose of contradicting each other? Are the passages really contradictory? If they are, the Bible is not a credible book. But does it not become the teachers of the various systems to, either expunge a part of these Scriptures, or harmonize them?

Why were these seeming contradictions written? The answer is not difficult. It was in consequence of the differences of the character of the persons addressed. Hence, to the jailer, the apostle said: "Believe," and the appropriateness of the direction is apparent from the fact, that he had not previously been instructed in the faith of Christ. Afterward, the apostles, "spoke the word of the Lord to the jailer and all that were in his house;" of course, they were taught the nature of belief and its evidence; and the consequence was, that the same hour of the night, all were baptized, and became rejoicing Christians. To the unbeliever, it would be altogether inappropriate to say, repent, pray or be baptized.

But if we have evidence of the existence of faith, it would be fanciful to say, believe. The Pentecostians had heard Peter preach the word, and, as evidence that they believed, they were "pricked in their heart," and cried, "Men and brethren, what shall we do?" The inspired Peter answered, "Repent." The most superficial reader can see the propriety of these different directions.

But suppose we could find an example of one who had believed with all his heart, and had repented of every sin, still was not a Christian, What should we direct him to do? We have a case in point. Saul of Tarsus, believed with his whole soul, the very moment he heard the voice from Heaven, "I am Jesus whom thou persecutest." From this instant, for three days, he neither ate nor drank anything, and all must agree that, during these sad hours, he not only had ample opportunity to reflect on his lost condition, but did, from the depths of his soul, repent of every sin. In this condition, it would have been foolish for Ananias to say, believe, repent, or pray, for he had believed, repented, and prayed. "What will you have me to do?" was the inquiry. Ananias approaches him to answer the prayer, and said: "Now why tarriest thou, arise and be baptized, and wash away thy sins, calling on the name of the Lord. Acts xxii, 16. There is, therefore, no contradiction in these Scriptures. Hence, the reader will at once see, and feel the necessity of understanding clearly the character of the persons addressed in the different parts of the Bible.

Rule VII. *The proper division of the Bible, should be constantly before the mind of the reader.*

Although this rule very nearly affiliates to the sixth, there are important bearings which somewhat differ, and under this head, we can introduce matter which does not seem so appropriate under the former.

The apostle, in giving the qualifications of an "approved workman," or preacher of the gospel, places the ability to "Rightly divide the work of truth," as an indispensable pre-requisite.

The reader will easily discover that, in the elucidation of this last, and in our judgment, most important rule for reading the Bible, we have before us a wide field for illustration.

In the first place, we beg leave to report a case, for the truth of which we are responsible. Years ago, in our travels, we spent a night at a town in a southern state, and heard the following conversation with the lady who presided at the supper table. She was asked:

"Are you a member of any church?" The lady in a feeble voice replied, "No." "Why are you not?" "I could not get religion." "Did you try?" "Yes," was the reply, "I tried several years, and when I saw many succeed so easily, I felt that there was none for me; and I have not prayed since." "Do you read the Bible?" said the fair inquirer. "Not now," said the woman, with a sad heart. "Why do you not read?" said she. "I cannot understand the Bible; and when I saw, many years ago, that I could not understand the Scriptures, I quit reading." The next question asked was; "What part of the Bible did you read, to learn how to become a Christian?" "Oh!" said the lady, "I was not particular; I found very pretty reading in Job, the Psalms, and more, I believe in Proverbs." The reader will discover that, this honest, yet deluded daughter of an old preacher, was looking up and down the Scriptures, hoping that she would, by chance, light upon some place that would show her how to "get religion." Her friends knew not how to direct her, and were, indeed, so shamefully ignorant that, they could not inform her; religion is not something which people "get," but a practice. James i, 26. She had no idea of the object of the books of the Old or New Testament, and presumed she would as likely learn how to become a Christian from the Proverbs of Solomon, the Psalms of David, or the distresses of poor, old, afflicted Job, as any part of the New Testament. Her father ought to have been able to teach her, that the Old Testament was not written for the purpose of giving information in reference to becoming the disciples of Jesus Christ.

Indeed, she ought to have known, that it was written long before Christ was born, or Christianity was revealed; and that Job, David and Solomon, all died looking for better things, but were not permitted to see the rising of the Sun of righteousness with healings in his wings.

If we are not mistaken, thousands of sincere persons read the Bible, with quite as much uncertainty as this good woman; and it is to them, so far as intelligence is concerned, a sealed book. Not many years since, she died, we are informed, as she had lived, without hope and without God.

If school teachers were to treat their pupils, as too many preachers and writers treat their congregations and readers, it would become a matter of grave deliberation, whether the schoolmaster should not be dismissed. Suppose the teacher, in opening his school, should require each pupil to bring all the books necessary to complete his education. The pupils, or perhaps the parents, would bring the 'Alphabetical Primer;' the 'Speller;' the various 'Readers;' the 'Grammar;' 'Geography;' 'Arithmetic;

perhaps 'Algebra,' 'Geometry,' etc., in the Mathematical line; a book on 'Chemistry;' another on 'Geology,' etc., etc., to the end of the course. We will witness this teacher's debut. Little John asks: "Mr. Schoolmaster, what shall I study?" The grave pedagogue replies; "You have all the books necessary to take you to Congress, and you may begin where you please, you have to study them all." Look at John, he has taken up 'Algebra,' wrong end up—hear him read;—that's fluent—a smart scholar he; but the poor little fellow does not know his letters, and of course, he can understand nothing in the book. This reminds us of members of the Romish Church, who read the service in Latin, without understanding a word that they read. But look round, and you will see the rest of the pupils in equal confusion. The more they study, the less they know,—their path grows darker and darker, and finally the disappointed children become weary, and throw down their books in disgust. "Mind your books," says the teacher; it is all to no effect, they cannot learn. What is the reason? The teacher began wrong, and years of labor on this plan, would be of no service. This, reader, is not an unapt illustration of reading the Scriptures.

The wise teacher will have his pupils begin at the alphabet, and proceed regularly and inductively, till they can master the highest branches. When one desires to study arithmetic, there is an appropriate book for the purpose; and no substitute will answer in its place. To learn grammar, geography, chemistry, etc., there are books entirely suitable. But we should remember that, geography cannot be learned from the treatise on algebra, neither can geology be learned from a treatise on music, and the best talent and closest application, will not enable students to surmount mistakes in selecting the books appropriate to the several departments of science.

These suggestions, it is hoped, will picture forth, the usual plan of studying religious subjects, and direct attention to a better plan. There is a proper beginning, and unless we start at the right point, we will miss the truth as far, as the clumsy surveyor, who would attempt to determine an amount of land, without a starting or concluding corner. The greater the labor, the greater the confusion in his plots.

A part of the Bible is appropriated to the Patriarchal religion; another part to the Jewish; and still, a third develops the Christian institution. These dispensations of divine wisdom, should be kept as separate as God has made them; and the books which treat of each, to be comprehended, must be read with direct reference to their respective subjects.

With these simple rules, we shall proceed to another, and still more interesting division of our subject.

PART THIRD.

THE BIBLE EXAMINED.

It would be unreasonable to conclude that, it is not in the power of accountable creatures, to acquire rich stores of spiritual light, by examining the sacred oracles; and we trust that, in our remaining investigations, our readers will contemplate the various points of discussion, with unvailed hearts.

I. What does the Bible purport to be?

The volume is usually called, "*The Bible*,"—meaning, "*The Book*," to express its pre-eminence over all other books; and it is believed by Christians that, it is the only volume on earth, which has God for its Author. The term Bible has been in use from an early age of the Christian Church; but from the close of the first century, the name "Holy Scriptures" has been employed to designate the contents of the Divine Volume.

As intimated, it purports to have been written by the inspiration of God. There are various theories of inspiration; but as our object is not so much a critical examination of the Scriptures, as to aid, particularly young persons, to read to advantage, we will barely introduce a few statements from the Bible itself, which afford, no doubt, the clearest view of the subject.

The apostle Paul tells us that, "God who at sundry times, and in divers manners, spake in times past unto the fathers by the prophets, hath in these last days spoken unto us by his Son." Heb. i, 1. Peter tells us that, "Holy men of God spake, as they were moved by the Holy Ghost." 2 Pet. i, 21. Christ told the apostles that, "The Spirit should 'guide' them into all truth;"—said He, "The Holy Spirit shall teach you all things, and bring all things to your remembrance, whatsoever I have said unto you." "It is not you that speak; but the Spirit of my Father that speaks in (through) you." The apostle to the Gentiles, asserted that, "Eye hath not seen, nor ear heard, neither have entered into the heart of man, the things which God hath prepared for them that love him. But God hath revealed them unto us by the Spirit. Which things also we speak not in the words which man's wisdom teacheth, but which the Holy Spirit teacheth; comparing spiritual things with spiritual." From these brief and lucid quotations, with scores of others equally pointed, we cannot doubt the inspiration of the Scriptures; and with Job, we exclaim, "There is a spirit in man, and the inspiration of the Almighty giveth them understanding."

As previously intimated, we believe the Bible contains all the information, in the least possible form, to make men wise unto salvation. That it is, in form and in fact, perfect in all its parts, and therefore, thoroughly furnishes the man of God, "with all things which pertain to life and godliness."

II. Languages in which the Bible was written.

The Old Testament was written in Hebrew, with the exception of parts of the books of Ezra, Nehemiah and Daniel, which were written in Chaldee.

The New Testament was written in the Greek Language, or what is called by the learned, Hellenistic or Hebraizing Greek. It is termed Hebraizing Greek, in consequence of various Hebrew words and forms of speech being incorporated in the composition. These, however, detract not from the strength or simplicity of the volume. The purest Greek of the New Testament, is said to be, the letter to the Hebrews; and the part containing the most Hebrew, is the Revelation.

III. The Translation.

The first English version of the entire Scriptures, was by John Wickliff, with the assistance of some friends, and was published about the year 1380 of our era. His

New Testament was published in 1367. Wickliff did not understand Hebrew or Greek, but being a good Latin scholar, he translated from the Vulgate or Latin version. Although there were many inaccuracies in this version, it was the means of shedding a flood of the pure light among the people.

William Tyndal, a Welchman by birth, but educated at Oxford, England, was banished from his native land for attempting to translate the Scriptures into a tongue which his countrymen could read ; but was enabled to give to the public his first edition of the New Testament in 1526. When copies were imported into England from Germany, where it was published, the Romish clergy were exceedingly provoked, and declared that, it was impossible to render the Scriptures into English; and still worse, that it was not lawful for the people to have them in their common tongue. They were displeased, likewise, because Tyndal, like Wickliff, had translated some of the *sacred words*, whose meaning they wished to hide from the people. It is probable, Tyndal translated mainly from the Latin Bible; as it was thought by many at that time, that, Latin was the most suitable language for the word of God; but he evidently compared it with the Greek, and it has been the basis of all English translations since his day. For the crime of giving the people the word of God, Tyndal was imprisoned in the castle at Antwerp in 1534 and in 1536; he was strangled and burnt as a heretic. ***Miles Canerdale***, while Tyndal was in prison, completed Tyndal's translation of the Old Testament, and gave the world the entire Bible in English in the year 1535.

Great Bible. In the year 1539, Grafton and Whitchurch published the English Bible, translated, as they declared in the title, by divers learned men, from the Hebrew and Greek. This is generally regarded as the first English translation from the originals.

Geneva Bible. On the death of Edward, King of England, Mary was raised to the throne, and her partisans were so severe against Protestants, that many took refuge in Germany, and at Geneva, some of them employed their time in translating the Scriptures. They published the New Testament in 1557. This is the first version of the New Testament, in which the verses of the chapters are distinguished by Numerical figures and breaks.

The Bishop's Bible. Queen Mary dying in 1558, was succeeded by Elizabeth, who restored the Protestant religion in England. In her reign Archbishop Parker, by the assistance of other Bishops of the English Church, published a revised version of the Bible in 1568. Hence it was called the Bishop's Bible.

King James's Bible. Queen Elizabeth dying in 1602, was succeeded by James VI., King of Scotland, who soon after his arrival at London, was petitioned by the Puritan ministers, to appoint a convention for the purpose of taking steps to prepare and publish a correct edition of the Scriptures ; and on the 12th of January, 1603, the Hampton Court conference convened. James appointed forty-seven translators for the work, to act in obedience to the following rules:

1st. "That they keep as close as possible to the Bishop's Bible."

2d. "That the names of the holy writers, be retained according to vulgar use."

3d. "That the old ecclesiastical words be kept, as the word *Church,* not to be translated Congregation."

4th. "That when a word has divers significations (which is impossible) that is to be kept, which has been most commonly used by the fathers." Or according to Lewis and Fuller, "Used by the most eminent fathers, being agreeable to the propriety of the place, and the analogy of faith."

Most of the other rules relate to the translators comparing notes and agreeing among themselves.

The translation was finished and published in 1611, and has been the only authorized version of the English Scriptures amongst Protestants for the space of 243 years.

As they labored under such embarrassing rules, the reader could scarcely look for a version free from error; but with all its defects in spelling, syntax, and failures to translate certain *ecclesiastical words*, the meaning of which they wished to keep from the people, it is, perhaps, the purest version in the English language.

That it needs amendments, no scholar denies; but still, most of the practical matters are so plain that, with proper rules for reading, the honest-hearted can scarcely fail learning the truth. Less than this, we could not say, and give the inquirer after truth, satisfaction in regard to the translation, which has been the standard of most of the pious of earth for so great a length of time.

IV. Divisions of the Bible.

The Old and New Testaments.

The Sacred Scriptures, in which are recorded the leading events of the world, from the creation for four thousand years, constitute what all Christians and Jews, call the "Old Testament." This is plain, from various passages found in the Bible. The apostle Paul says: (2 Cor. iii, 14), "For until this day the same vail is untaken away in reading the Old Testament." In

(Heb. ix, 15), he again speaks of "the first testament." The books authorized by Jesus Christ, are called "The New Testament." The Saviour says: (Mat. xxvi, 28), "This is my blood of the New Testament." Paul says: (2 Cor. iii, 6), "He made us able ministers of the New Testament." Also, (Heb. vii, 22), "Was Jesus made a surety of a better testament." Heb. ix, 15. "He is the mediator of the New Testament."

Each of these respective documents, is often designated by the word *covenant* in our translation. "Behold, the days come, saith the Lord, when I will make a new covenant with the house of Israel, and with the house of Judah. Not according to the covenant that I made with their fathers, . . . because they continued not in my covenant." Heb. viii, 9.

Jesus Christ is said to be, "The mediator of a better covenant, established upon better promises. For if that first covenant had been faultless, then no place should have been sought for the second." Heb. viii, 6, 7, 8.

By way of contrast, the Old Testament is called, "The ministration of death," "The ministration of condemnation," whilst the New is styled, "The ministration of righteousness," and "The ministration of the spirit." In consequence of the inefficiency of the Old Testament, it is called simply, "The letter,"—"The letter killeth," whilst the New, in consequence of the superior spiritual blessings which are enjoyed, is styled, "The spirit,"—"The spirit giveth life." 2 Cor. iii, 6–9. It is our purpose first, to examine, particularly,

The Divisions of the Old Testament.

The New Testament writers speak plainly of "*The law, the prophets and the psalms*," but all these are comprehended in the general term, "Scriptures." In the Old Testament, there are thirty-nine books or treatises, and it is a singular fact that, no two of these were written with precisely the same design. The following is, perhaps, the most perspicuous and satisfactory division of these most ancient and sacred documents:

1st. HISTORY or LAW.
2d. PROPHESY, — PROPHETS.
3d. POETRY, — PSALMS, etc.

Of the thirty-nine books of the Old covenant, *eighteen* are history, *sixteen* are prophetical, and *five* are purely poetical. It is true, there are parts of prophecies, which are poetical, but our divisions are sufficiently accurate for practical purposes.

In the historical parts of the Old Testament, we begin with Genesis, and conclude with Job; and, as we wish the reader to believe that, all these historic books are sufficiently plain to be understood by those who are able to read, we will call attention to some of the striking features of a few of them, with the hope that, the student will, in like manner, be encouraged to examine all the books.

Scholars admit that, Moses was the author of Genesis, Exodus, Leviticus, Numbers, and Deuteronomy; and that, God commissioned him to write them. It is a well ascertained fact that, he was born about 2,400 years after the creation, and lived a hundred and twenty years.

The first book of his composition is called GENESIS, in Greek, from the Hebrew, *Bereshith*, which means the *beginning*. The word Genesis, implies origin, source, creation, etc., and the most commonly received idea is, that it is the book descriptive of the Creation.

The very first verse of the book, gives an exalted view of the character of Jehovah. Whilst the ignorant had speculated most wildly in reference to the origin of the earth, man, the heavens, and all animate and inanimate objects. Moses says: "In the beginning (first of all) God created the heavens and the earth." In other words God is the author of the universe. The idea of so vast a creation from nothing, is one of the grandest conceptions that ever filled the soul of man. After the heavens and the earth had received the impress of Majesty, six days were required, for arranging the agencies of the universe, and creating the vegetables and animals of the earth; and the last and noblest earthly creation, was man, from the dust of the ground; and the most refined portion, was woman, from a rib of the man. Adam, with his pure and lovely Eve, was placed in the garden of delights, "to dress and keep it;" and as he had been created with no capacity for self-government, the Heavenly Father, revealed to him a government, in obedience to which he might live happily, but as a penalty for disobedience, his Creator told him that, in the day he transgressed, "he should surely die." Gen. ii, 16. The devil persuaded Eve that there was no force in law, and she was free to follow what seemed good in her own eyes. Being deceived, she "was in the transgressions," and in consequence of Adam's hearkening to the voice of his wife, he likewise became a sinner. These previously innocent and pure persons, who had never experienced the least pain or remorse, fell from their purity under the curse of mortality. Their punishment is thus expressed: "Unto the woman he said, I will greatly multiply thy sorrow, and thy conception, in sorrow thou shalt bring forth children; and thy desire shall be to thy husband, and he shall rule over thee. And unto Adam he said, because thou hast hearkened unto the voice of thy wife, and hast eaten of the tree of which I commanded thee, saying, Thou shalt not eat of it; cursed is the ground for thy sake; in sorrow shalt thou eat of it all the days of thy life. Thorns also and thistles shall it bring forth to thee, and thou shalt eat the herb of the field. In the sweat of thy face shalt thou eat bread, till thou return unto the ground; for out of it wast thou taken; for dust thou art and unto dust shalt thou return." Gen. iii, 16–19.

For their sins, "The Lord God sent them forth from the garden of Eden to till the ground;" and placed a flaming sword to guard the way of the tree of life, to prevent them from eating the fruit thereof and becoming eternal sinners.

Misfortunes were not staid at this sad catastrophe. Cain, the first born of this once happy pair, from a feeling of envy, killed his brother Abel; and for his sin, was made a wanderer and traveler in the earth. About fifteen hundred years after the Creation, as men were multiplied in the earth, they so "corrupted their way" that

Jehovah determined to destroy the whole race, save the single family of Noah. This faithful man, with his three sons, and their wives, spent a hundred and twenty years in preparations,—the ark was completed,—and the family entered it with "clean beasts and beasts that were not clean, and fowls and every creeping thing upon the earth." Then "God broke up the fountains of the great deep, and the windows of heaven were opened," and the rain poured down for the space of forty days and forty nights, till the water stood fifteen cubits above the highest mountains. "All that was on the dry land perished." At the end of a hundred and fifty days, the waters abated, and the ark rested on the mountains of Ararat. After a voyage of twelve months, Noah and his family, with their flocks, went forth from the ark, and built an altar to the Lord, and God blessed Noah and his sons, and said, "be fruitful and multiply and replenish the earth." Some two hundred years after the flood, the Heavenly Father called Abraham, and made to him two singularly great promises; the first was, that his family should become not only a great nation, but should continue an eternal monument of truth to the world; and secondly that, out of this nation, should one arise to save all who would put their trust in Him. Hence Paul says: "To Abraham were the promises made."

Abraham was the father of Isaac, and Isaac was the father of Jacob, who was the father of the twelve patriarchs. These patriarchs, in consequence of a grievous famine in the land of Canaan, moved into Egypt, and were made bondmen for the space of four hundred years. During this state of bondage, the children of Israel were greatly oppressed, and their cries and prayers ascended up to heaven. But Jacob died, and Joseph, his son, who had been the agent in the hands of God, in preserving his kindred from starvation, also died, being a hundred and ten years old. Before his death, however, he took an oath from his brethren, saying: "you shall carry up my bones from hence." "His body was embalmed and put into a coffin in Egypt."

Thus ends the first book of the Bible,

and if the reader will examine it closely, he will discover that it affords a very perfect history of our world for the space of twenty-three hundred years. This introduces us to

The Second Book of Moses, called

Exodus.—The Title, though uninspired, gives the main idea of the book. The word Exodus, is composed of two Greek words, *ex*, from, and *odus*, a way, and literally means, a going out, or departure.

It opens with the birth of Moses, who, to contravene a law of Egypt, requiring the male children of the Hebrews to be put to death, was concealed by his mother three months, and when she saw the life of herself and family was endangered by this procedure, "She took for him an ark of bulrushes, and daubed it with slime and with pitch, and put the child therein, and she laid it in the flags by the river side." Ex. ii, 3.

When the king's daughter "came down to wash at the river, she saw the ark among the flags, and sent her maid to fetch it." "And when she had opened it, she saw the child, and behold the babe wept." She determined to preserve it, and his mother was brought as nurse. This Moses was trained up in all the learning of the Egyptians, and when he was about forty years old, he saw the Egyptians imposing upon some of his brethren amongst the Hebrews, and he was so exasperated, that he slew one of them. For this offense, he fled from the country, and "dwelt in the land of Midian," where, for his gallantry in assisting certain maidens to water their father's flock, he won the heart of Zipporah, the daughter of Reuel, priest of the country. At the end of forty years, being eighty years old, Jehovah made known to him his determination to deliver the children of Israel from bondage, by speaking to him from a burning bush on Mt. Horeb. With his brother Aaron, he assembled the elders of the Jewish nation, and acquainted them with the gracious design of Heaven. Soon after, they had an interview with Pharaoh, king of Egypt, and requested permission for the people to hold a feast to their God in the wilderness. The king not only refused, but doubled their burdens. In answer to the prayer of Moses, Jehovah informed him that he would, "rid him out of their bondage, and would redeem the people with a stretched-out arm and with great judgments." Ex. iii.

Then followed a series of notable miracles, called "the Plagues of Egypt;" and finally the king being overcome—the first-born of all his people being slain by the angel of death, he consented to let the people of God go. On the night of the self-same day, which terminated a period of 430 years, after entering Egypt, 600,000 adult Israelites, "beside children, and a mixed multitude also went up with them; and flocks and herds, even very much cattle." Ex. xii, 37, 38. They left the rich plains of Goshen and traveled eastward in the direction of the Red Sea. They journeyed day and night, and "the Lord went before them by day in a pillar of cloud to lead them by the way, and by night, in a pillar of fire to give them light." Ex. xiii, 17. The design of Jehovah was evidently to conduct them to the most difficult place for crossing the sea; for he said: "I will be honored upon Pharaoh and upon all his hosts, that the Egyptians may know that I am the Lord." With this object, they approached the sea between vast mountains. Ex. xiv, 2–4. No sooner had Pharaoh learned that his slaves had fled, and were in perils on the sea-shore, than he summoned his troops and set out in hot pursuit. "He overtook them encamping by the sea, beside Pi-hahiroth before Baal-zephon." Here, "The angel of God which went before the camp of Israel, removed and went behind, and the pillar of the cloud went from before their face, and stood behind them, and it came between the camp of the Egyptians and the camp of Israel, and it was a cloud and darkness to them, but it gave light by night to these; so that the one came not near the other all the night." Ex. xiv, 19, 20.

Here it was, the whole congregation wept most bitterly, and even the great heart of Moses began to sink within him, and in his fear and bitterness of soul, he said to the people, "Stand still and see the salvation of the Lord." But the Lord said unto

Moses, "Wherefore criest thou unto me? Speak unto the children of Israel, that they go forward. But lift thou up the rod, and stretch out thy hand over the sea, and divide it. And Moses stretched out his hand over the sea; and the Lord caused the sea to go back by a strong east wind all that night, and made the sea dry land, and the waters were divided. And the children of Israel went into the midst of the sea upon the dry ground; and the waters were a wall unto them on their right-hand and on their left. Ex. xiv. The Egyptians pursued after them into the sea, and "The Lord took off their chariot-wheels, that they draw them heavily; and they said, Let us flee from the face of Israel, for the Lord fighteth for them." The Lord commanded Moses to "stretch out his hand over the sea, that the waters may come again upon the Egyptians." He did so, and "the sea returned to his strength, when the morning appeared, and the waters returned and covered the chariots and the horsemen, and all the host of Pharaoh that came into the sea after them; there remained not so much as one of them;

thus the Lord saved Israel that day out of the hand of the Egyptians; and the people feared the Lord, and his servant Moses."

"Then sang Moses and the children of Israel unto the Lord, saying, I will sing unto the Lord, for he hath triumphed gloriously; the horse and his rider hath he thrown into the sea. The Lord is my strength and song, and he is become my salvation; he is my God, and I will prepare Him a habitation." Thus baptized into Moses by the cloud and sea, the children of Israel journeyed to Mt. Sinai, where the Lord said: "Ye have seen what I have done unto the Egyptians, and how I have you on eagles' wings, and brought you to myself. Now if you will obey my voice, indeed, and keep my covenant, then you shall be a peculiar treasure unto me above all people. And you shall be unto me a kingdom of priests and a holy nation." And the people said: "All that the Lord hath spoken, we will do."

From the mountain, the Lord delivered the law for the children of Israel on two tables of stone. In addition to the ten commandments, He gave full regulations, concerning property, life and all the conduct of the nation. In these laws, Jehovah directed the order of worship, and authorized Moses to make a tabernacle in which alone was his service to be performed. The work was completed under the direction of Bezaleel and Aholiab, men who were "wise-hearted," and "filled with the spirit of God."

When the tabernacle was finished, all the vessels and furniture were placed in it, as the Lord directed, and "A cloud covered the tent of the congregation, and the glory of the Lord filled the tabernacle." Thus it was owned as God's house; and "the cloud was on the tabernacle by day, and fire was on it by night, in the sight of all the house of Israel, throughout all their journeys." And thus closes Exodus, the second book of Moses, all the contents of which are intimately connected with the trials of the family of Abraham, and, indeed, the first church of the Living God, on earth.

THE THIRD BOOK OF MOSES, CALLED LEVITICUS.—In the Hebrew canon, it is called *bayekra*, and signifies, *to call;* perhaps, from the first verse of the book, in which it is said, "The Lord called unto Moses, and spoke unto him out of the tabernacle."

The subject-matter pertains, mainly, to instructions of the priests, the sons of Levi.

It contains fuller statements and developments of the tabernacle-worship than is found in the book of Exodus. It begins, indeed, by describing the worship itself, and the first seven chapters are devoted chiefly to the Jewish sacrifices. In the eighth and ninth chapters, we have directions for consecrating Aaron and his sons to the priest's office. As we proceed through the book, *holy* and *unholy* things are minutely described.

The great feast of Atonement, formed the central point of the nation's sanctity; for by it, all the people were reconciled to God. The sixteenth chapter ends with this declaration: "And this shall be an everlasting statute unto you, to make an atonement for the children of Israel, for all their sins once a year."

Most of the other chapters, to the close of the book, are intended to guard the priests and the people against the influence of all foreign religions, and the proper motives for separating themselves from other nations, are clearly, and most forcibly set forth.

The details, however, are full of interest, and we would urge upon the reader the importance of studying the entire book with care.

NUMBERS, or the fourth book of Moses, gets its title from the fact, that, the children of Israel were numbered in the wilderness for the purpose of separating the Levites from such as had to bear arms. In Hebrew, it is called, *be-midbar*, which means, *in the wilderness.*

Many of the most important events which occurred with the Jews during their forty years in the desert, are faithfully described in this book, and the narrative conducts us to "The plains of Moab by Jordan near Jericho."

Deuteronomy, is the fifth and last book of Moses, and the title indicates, "a second publishing of the Law." It is a rehearsal of all that God had spoken by Moses, and contains, in addition, many earnest exhortations, and sublime prophecies. When Moses wrote it, he was anxious to look to the future—the world was fading from his vision—and, indeed, it may be called his farewell address to the people who had followed him during his forty years' journey from Egypt.

He ascended the mountain of Nebo, opposite Jericho, to the top of Pisgah, from whose summit he could view the long-promised land. Although he was a hundred and twenty years old, "his eye was not dim, nor his natural force abated." Here he died, and was buried in one of the valleys. The children of Israel wept for him thirty days. The balance of the eighteen historical books of the Old Testamant are equally plain; still the valuable instructions contained in each, can be acquired only by diligent and prayerful study.

This division ends with the history of faithful Job, who, though forsaken by his friends—deprived of his property, and most that seemed dear, could exclaim: "The Lord gave and the Lord hath taken away, blessed be the name of the Lord. In all this Job sinned not, nor charged God foolishly."

As previously intimated, the second division of the Old Testament, is composed of SIXTEEN PROPHETICAL BOOKS.

An exposition of these, in the general application of the term, would be an arduous undertaking. Indeed, it is not suitable for a work intended, mainly, for such as are but beginners in the Heavenly science.

Our object will be fully accomplished, by barely calling attention to the character of the prophets, and the proper idea of a prediction.

Prophets were not necessarily lawgivers, though Moses was both a lawgiver and a prophet. Most of them were men inspired by the spirit of God, to rouse a slumbering nation to a sense of danger. We usually, however, understand by a prophet, one who was endowed with power to foretell with infallible certainty, future events.

These predictions of events, made hundreds of years before they came to pass, prove themselves miraculous in their accomplishment.

The prophecies concerning the preservation of the Jewish nation, are regarded as a perpetual miracle in favor of inspiration. The greatest wonder in the whole subject, consists in the well established fact that, the most unreasonable and incongruous events which were foretold, have been fulfilled to the very letter.

Many of the prophecies from Isaiah to Malachi have had their completion; but there are others in reference to the Jews, particularly, and the final triumphs of Christ's kingdom, yet to be accomplished.

They cannot be studied as simple narratives, for their style, in places, from being highly metaphorical, approaches very nearly to poetical composition. Yet most persons will derive signal advantage from perusing and carefully studying the prophecies.

The Poetry of the Bible, or our Third Division of the Old Testament.

While it is admitted that, most of the books of the Old Testament contain passages highly poetical, all agree that the Psalms of David, Proverbs, Ecclesiastes and Song of Solomon, and Lamentations of Jeremiah, are highly poetical. Our advice on this division will be brief.

The word Psalms, is derived from the Greek *Psalmai*, and it from *Psalto*, to strike a chord.

David and his associates chanted, or sung these compositions, to stringed and other instruments of music.

The principal idea of Proverbs, is taken from the meaning of the word, *similitude* or *comparison;* and the reader will observe that, the object of the writer, was to give practical and authoritative maxims, in highly figurative language.

The word Ecclesiastes, implies a composition for the whole congregation of the Lord.

The Song of Solomon or Canticles, signifies, the song of songs, which implies the superior beauty and excellence of the poem.

THE LAMENTATIONS OF JEREMIAH. This book is sometimes called TEARS, "in allusion to the mournful character of the work, of which one would conceive," says Bishop Lowth, "that every letter was written with a tear,—every word the sound of a broken heart." No doubt, it was written by the prophet in the bitterest anguish of his soul, to express the mournful condition of himself and his people in consequence of transgression.

Our limits forbid a further examination of the first division of the Bible, and we close by enjoining it upon the reader, to endeavor to get the chief thought, or subject-matter, in examining these most ancient, sacred, and valuable compositions of antiquity.

THE NEW TESTAMENT.

The New Testament contains the revelations of God to the world by his Son, through the apostles, and faithful and inspired men, chosen for the purpose of making known his will to the nations. It will be remembered that, the Old Testament was intended mainly for the Jews; but a little over eighteen hundred and fifty years ago, "God sent forth his son, made of a woman, made under the law, to redeem them that were under the law," (Gal. iv, 4); that both Jews and Gentiles might receive the adoption of sons by faith in Christ Jesus.

By him, "a new and living way" was set forth, and all people, tongues and tribes were invited to walk therein, says the apostle: "For he is our peace, who hath made both one, and hath broken down the middle wall of partition between us; having abolished in his flesh, the enmity, even the law of commandments contained in ordinances; for to make in himself of twain, one new man (or church) so making peace; and that he might reconcile both unto God in one body by the cross, having slain the enmity thereby, and came and preached peace to you (Gentiles) who were afar off, and to them (Jews) who were nigh. For through him we both have access, by one spirit unto the Father. Now, therefore, you (Gentiles) are no more strangers and foreigners, but fellow-citizens with the saints and of the household of God; and are built upon the foundation of the apostles and prophets, Jesus Christ himself being the chief corner-stone. In whom all the building, fitly framed together, groweth unto a holy temple in the Lord; in whom you also are builded together for a habitation of God through the spirit." Eph. ii, 14–22.

Inasmuch as our reading and investigations are always interesting in proportion to the importance of the subject we are examining, we should endeavor to get a clear idea of the Christian institution.

Primitively, apostles and other inspired men, delivered whole discourses in regard to "the kingdom of God, and the name of Jesus Christ;" but if a minister in the nineteenth century were to select such a subject for a sermon, his auditors would be greatly surprised. Yet the kingdom of God, or church of Christ, is the burden of the New Testament. God promised in the Old Testament times, that, he would "set up a kingdom that should stand forever." John the Baptist, said: "The kingdom of heaven is at hand." Jesus our Saviour, exhorted to "Pray, thy kingdom come," and when Peter made the confession of the leading and center truth of Christianity, that "Jesus was the Christ the Son of the living God," he announced that, "On this rock"—confession—"I will build my church, and the gates of hell shall not prevail against it." This new kingdom, which was not "of this world," was always mentioned as "coming," as being "at hand," till the Holy Spirit acknowledged the body at Jerusalem on the day of Pentecost.

Previously to this day, we have no mention of persons being added to, or joining the Church—all was before preparation—the materials for the spiritual building were "made ready" by John, and by Jesus Christ and his apostles. But no sooner had the spirit descended and the three thousand added to the disciples, than "the Lord added to the church daily the saved;" or as it reads in our version, "such as should be saved." Acts ii, 47. Thus was the kingdom established amongst the Jews, and it soon spread through Samaria, and some seven years afterward, it was set up among the Gentiles at the house of Cornelius.

We rejoice also to know that, for more than eighteen hundred years, this kingdom has stood as a city on a hill, with doors open to all who would enter the fold of God. The young reader should understand very clearly that, no one can enjoy the rich blessings of this spiritual empire, who refuses allegiance to the king. The Saviour compared the kingdom to a vineyard, and said the Master went out to hire laborers, early, at the sixth, ninth, and eleventh hour, but the condition of service in every instance was, to "go into the vineyard." Whoever will be the disciple of Jesus, must renounce himself, his own wisdom and plans, and all the plans of men, and take up his cross and follow him.

Christ invites the weary and heavy laden to "come to Him," to "learn of Him," and to "take His yoke" in order to have rest.

The glory of the Christian religion is its transcendent spirituality over all other religions. The Jewish institutions failed to purify:—"There was a remembrance of sin made every year"—"It was impossible for the blood of bulls and goats to take away sin," but Christ, in entering into the holy place by his own blood, has obtained "eternal redemption for us," and we now have the promise of the Father that, "Our sins and iniquities shall be remembered against us no more." In this spiritual institution, the eternal life and immortality were "brought to light," of which the world had remained profoundly ignorant for four thousand years.

It is by means of this Church, God can be honorable and honored in saving all sinners who will come to Him through the mediator, Christ Jesus. "There is no other name by which we can be saved."

Eternal honor in the future depends upon the acknowledgment of Christ's authority; and he that refuses is threatened with banishment from the presence of the Lord, and the glory of his power.

Of the salvation by Jesus Christ, there are no books which directly and authoritatively treat, save those in the New Testament. We are happy also to know these sacred productions, constitute an infallible system or *creed*, and forever settle every controversy.

It may be some satisfaction for the young reader to understand, that these books were all written during the first century of the Christian era, and have afforded the only spiritual light which the world has enjoyed since the apostle John died. We are forbidden to anticipate or look for other light. Indeed, the very fact of praying for, or professing to receive additional information with regard to the spiritual world, is positive evidence that we are neither satisfied or pleased with what we have, and what God intended should be the only light in the pathway of life. With these introductory remarks and plain statements, we proceed to examine

THE DIVISIONS OF THE NEW TESTAMENT.

There are in this purest volume of earth, twenty-seven books or treatises, each of which, was written for a specified object, and from their matter, they may be divided into four classes, or chapters.

1st. The Gospel.

2d. The Book of Conversions.

3d. The Book of Discipline.

4th. The Book of Revelations.

We hope the kind reader will not conclude that, our divisions are novel or unmeaning. A little patience in examining the volume, will enable the inquirer to see that, these have been made by the sacred writers themselves, and, moreover, that the very matter, and subjects, not only suggest, but demand them. We will examine these heads in order.

I. The Gospel.

Superficial readers, who expect to find the Gospel of Christ scattered promiscuously through the whole of the Bible, will not be likely to find it anywhere. Christian people regard all the Bible as the word of God, but all the word of God, is not the Gospel of Jesus Christ, who was not born till the year 4004. The history of the flood, for instance, in the days of good Noah, though true, contains not the Gospel; neither do we find it in the Law, the Prophets, or

Psalms in detail. To be sure, reference was made by divers Old Testament writers, to things which were to occur and which have since taken place, and which, by the New Testament writers, were called Gospel. On this point the apostle Paul informs us that, "Unto us was the Gospel preached as well as unto them, but the word preached did not profit them, not being mixed with faith in them that heard it." Heb. iv, 2.

This translation does not give the apostle's meaning with sufficient fairness. In the original, there is no article in connection with the word Gospel, and the following is the literal reading. "For unto us were glad tidings preached, as well as to them." Again Peter tells us, (1 Peter iv, 6); "Good news,"—not, "the Gospel," as in our version—was preached to the dead, that is, to the antediluvians who are now dead; but this 'good news,' doubtless, reached them through the preaching of righteous Noah, before their death.

To the Galatians, Paul says: "The Scriptures foreseeing that God would justify the heathen through faith, preached before the Gospel (literally translated *Gospel*) unto Abraham, saying, In thee shall all nations be blessed." Gal. iii, 8. With these Scriptures before us, it is quite apparent, that the promise to Abraham of a coming Saviour was denominated good news, glad tidings, concerning a Deliverer—Gospel. The student of the Bible will also discover, that this was a *prospective* Gospel, or a Gospel only in promise. Scores of the faithful, from the time the promise of the Messiah was made to Abraham, anxiously looked for an illustrious person to appear, as a king and preserver of the nation. The announcement that such an one would come, was styled, Gospel, or glad tidings to be realized in the future. The whole thought is beautifully expressed by Paul, in his letter to the Hebrews. In speaking of the faithful of old, he said: "These all died in faith, not having received the promises, but having seen them afar off, and were persuaded by them, and embraced them, and confessed that, they were strangers and pilgrims on the earth." Heb. xi, 13.

We see then, in what sense the Gospel was preached to the people before the birth of Christ, and we are now fully prepared to connect all the facts of the Gospel of our salvation, with Him, who "came down from heaven not to do his own will, but the will of Him that sent Him."

It may be proper to add that, the whole Gospel in all its facts and practical bearings, was not, and could not be preached, till after the resurrection of our Lord from the dead; and, indeed, till after the ascension, and the descent of the Holy Spirit on the day of Pentecost.

The word Gospel implies glad tidings, good news; as appears from the announcement of the angel to the shepherd, who were vigilantly watching their flocks on the Judean hills, the night in which the Saviour was born. "The angel said unto them, fear not: for, behold, I bring you glad tidings of great joy which shall be to all people. For unto you is born this day in the city of David, a Saviour, who is Christ the Lord." Luke ii, 11, 12.

This Gospel is construed by many learned men, to mean, *God's spell*, means or power, to bring the erring back to their Father's house; but the apostle gives concisely the facts of the Gospel to the Corinthians. He says: "Moreover, brethren, I declared unto you the Gospel which I preached unto you, which also, you have received, and wherein you stand.

"By which also you are saved, if you keep in memory what I preached unto you, unless you have believed in vain. For I delivered unto you, first of all, that which I also received; how that Christ died for our sins according to the Scriptures; and that he was buried; and that he rose again the third day according to the Scriptures." 1 Cor. xv, 1–4.

Whoever reads to profit, will readily discover that, the Gospel which he preached and in which the Corinthians "stood," and by which they "were saved," contained three very clear and distinct items:

1st. "*Christ died for our sins according to the Scriptures.*"

2d. "*He was buried.*"

3d. "*He was raised from the dead the third day according to the Scriptures.*"

In all the discourses of the inspired ambassadors of the Saviour, after his resurrection, these were the prominent and reliable facts, preached for the conversion of men to God. Moreover, every infidel that has assailed the religion of Jesus Christ, has made his attacks at this impregnable fortress. That Jesus of Nazareth lived in Judea at the time reported by his witnesses, and that he died by the authority of a warrant from Pontius Pilate, the Roman governor of the province of Judea, even the enemies, in all time since, have freely admitted; and consequently, the only point in controversy to fully establish Christianity is, did Jesus Christ rise from the dead as reported? That it is against nature and contrary to all the logic and philosophy of men, we freely admit; but the very admission—and none will refuse to make it—that man did not *happen* on the earth, but is the creation of One who is above creation, concedes all that the Christian religion demands. Grant that God is, and the miraculous delivery of our Saviour from the tomb, is also admitted. True, we have not demonstrable evidence of the resurrection, and we should not ask it, for this would be walking "by sight and not by faith." We are to believe that Christ rose from the dead upon the authority of men who sacrificed all worldly honor and died, not for opinions, or strong persuasion, but for telling the truth in regard to what they *saw and heard of the Lord.*

In the great commission, the chosen of heaven, were commanded to preach this Gospel; and no one has charged them with unfaithfulness. They not only preached, "Jesus Christ and him crucified," but such as believed, "with all the heart unto righteousness, made the confession with the mouth unto salvation."

In the Gospel of our salvation, we observe nothing resembling a party system of religion, a partisan creed, or any important fact which can be misunderstood. Though simple in its statements, there is a majesty in every declaration which cannot fail to fill the soul with awe and devotion. But the main object of our inquiry, after setting forth plainly the meaning, matter, and intention of the Gospel, is to ascertain in what books it is contained.

We have often heard clerks, justices of the peace, and lawyers speak of swearing men "on the four Gospels," or "Holy Evangelists," meaning neither all the Bible nor all of the New Testament. When one is sworn on these four books, without reference to any other portion, it is agreed the person has taken a Gospel oath.

While we might mention with due respect, that the phrase, "Four Gospels," is not critically correct, it is a most singular and significant truth that, men who speak of the Gospel with an untheological intent, are usually more accurate in their style, than many sticklers for party systems.

In the early ages of the Church, this Gospel of the Son of God, not really "four Gospels," but this single everlasting Gospel, written by the four servants of God, Matthew, Mark, Luke, and John, formed a separate and independent volume. All acquainted with church history, are aware that, in primitive times, these books were preserved in a distinct form for the purpose of giving the most perspicuous conception of their character. We believe it would be far better for the present generation, to study the Gospel set forth, disconnected from all the other books of the Bible.

The plan would at least save the young mind from much confusion on the subject of searching the Scriptures. Irenæus, an ancient father of the Church, speaks of the Gospel as "the one four-formed, or four-sided Gospel." But can we be mistaken in our position, that these books contain, emphatically, the Gospel in all its fullness and details, which cannot be found elsewhere?

It will be in keeping with our design, and we hope, with the design of the reader, to briefly notice the contents of these books.

Matthew opens his narrative with the genealogy of our Saviour Jesus Christ. He traces His family from Abraham to Joseph, the husband of Mary, who was the mother of our Lord, through a space of nearly two thousand years.

Luke, in his genealogical table, begins with Jesus, whom he calls the son of Heli, and traces back to Adam the Son of God. In a part of these family tables, there seems to be a contradiction, which, perhaps, will disappear, if we admit with Dr. Barrett, Olshansen and others, that Matthew relates the history of Joseph through his real father Jacob, and Luke, gives the history of Mary, the mother of our Lord, through Heli, who was the father-in-law of Joseph. Both narratives then, are correct. Jacob was the father of Joseph after the flesh, but as Joseph was not, in fact, the father of Jesus, he was acknowledged the lawful father, because he was the husband of Mary, the daughter of Heli. They both unite at David, and one traces through Solomon, and the other through Nathan. This brief statement seems to us, to remove the discrepancy. But there is perfect agreement, that our Lord was born in Bethlehem, near Jerusalem, according to the prophecy.

Matthew details the conception and birth of the Saviour, as follows: "When as his mother Mary was esuoused to Joseph, before they came together, she was found with child of the Holy Spirit." The matter being explained to Joseph's satisfaction, by an angel, he "took unto him his wife;" "and she brought forth her first-born son, and he called his name Jesus." Matt. i, 18–25. Soon after his birth, Jesus, in consequence of Herod seeking his life, was taken by Joseph and Mary into Egypt, where he remained until the death of Herod, when an angel directed Joseph to "take the young child again into the land of Israel." And he arose and took the young child and his mother, and came into the land of Israel. But when he heard that, Archelaus did reign in Judea, in the room of his father Herod, he was afraid to go thither, and he turned aside into the parts of Galilee, and he came and dwelt in a city called Nazareth.

We have no further account of his childhood by any of the writers, except Luke. He informs us that, "When he was twelve years old, they went up to Jerusalem after the custom of the feast. And when they had fulfilled the days, as they returned, the child Jesus tarried behind in Jerusalem, and Joseph and His mother knew not of it." "At the end of three days they found Him in the temple, sitting in the midst of the doctors, both hearing them, and asking them questions. And all that heard Him, were astonished at His understanding and answers. And when they saw Him, they were amazed: and his mother said unto Him, Son, why hast thou thus dealt with us? Behold thy father and I have sought thee sorrowing. And He said, Know ye not, that I must be about my Father's business?"

"And He went down with them and came to Nazareth, and was subject unto them; but His mother kept all these sayings in her heart. And Jesus increased in wisdom and stature and in favor with God and man." Luke iii, 41-52. We have no additional information on the subject, till He was about thirty years of age; but before proceeding with the personal narrative of our Lord, it would be well for the reader to examine the character and mission of John the Baptizer, or Baptist, as the word is erroneously given in our version.

This good man and prophet of God, was a relation of our Saviour, and was sent before Him, "To prepare his ways; to give the knowledge of salvatiou by the remission of sins. To give light to them that sat in darkness and in the shadow of death, to guide their feet in the way of peace." Luke i, 76–79.

This John was "clothed with camel's hair, and wore a leathern girdle about his loins, and his meat was locusts and wild honey." He went crying through the wilderness of Judea and along the banks of the Jordan, "Repent ye, for the kingdom of heaven is at hand." "He was the voice of one crying in the wilderness, prepare ye the way of the Lord, make his paths straight."

The effort of this simple, yet earnest preaching, was most wonderful, as appears, from the narratives. Mark says: "John did baptize in the wilderness, and preach the baptism of repentance for the remission of sins.

"And there went out to him all the land of Judea, and they of Jerusalem, and were all baptized of him in the river Jordan, confessing their sins." When John saw that, his ministry was becoming dangerously popular, he denounced his flatterers as a "Generation of vipers," and demanded of them fruits as evidence of their repentance.

He informed the Jews, that, "One so far above him, that he was not worthy to stoop down and untie his shoes, would soon come and baptize with the Holy Spirit and fire." He said to them: "The ax is laid unto the root of the trees; therefore, every tree which bringeth not forth good fruit, is hewn down and cast into the fire."

"The wheat," or good, were to be taken into the garner; but the chaff he was to punish with a baptism of "unquenchable fire." At thirty years of age, Jesus was baptized of John in the river Jordan, and He "went up straightway out of the water; and lo, the heavens were opened unto Him, and He saw the Spirit of God, descending like a dove and lighting upon Him. And lo, a voice from heaven, saying, "This is my beloved Son in whom I am well pleased."

Matt. iii, 17. Then Jesus was tempted of Satan forty days in the wilderness; and when his temptations were ended, He called twelve disciples whom He ordained and sent forth to preach his approaching kingdom. These apostles were forbidden to go to the Gentiles, but were to confine their labors to "the lost sheep of the house of Israel." When the disciples had sufficiently multiplied, he chose seventy, and sent them out, two and two, to preach that the kingdom was at hand. Signs and wonders followed the Messiah's labors to such a marvelous extent, that when some of his disciples returned to Him, and reported what they had done, he said: "I saw Satan as lightning fall from heaven." In all our Lord's travels, his object was the good of men. "The blind eyes were opened, the deaf ears were unstopped, the lame leaped for joy, the tongue of the dumb sang the high praises of God, and better than all, the poor heard the Gospel's joyful sound. Most happy was he pronounced who was not offended at the Lord's miracles and teaching."

This "carpenter" and son of a carpenter, fearlessly reproved sin in high places, regardless of sneers and persecutions. He came on earth, indeed, to wage eternal war against vice, and while he threatened destruction to the hard hearted, he graciously held out the scepter of pardon and peace to all who would come to God by Him.

Though He never did harm, neither was guile found on his lips, He "was despised and rejected of men," and was, emphatically, "a man of sorrows and acquainted with grief." Earthly possessions He had none. "The foxes have holes," said He, "and the birds of the air have nests, but the Son of man hath no place to lay his head." This is He, who had been "rich in heaven, but for our sakes became poor, that we through his poverty might be rich." He "came down from heaven not to do his own will, but the will of his Father who sent Him." Still He advocated no violent measures to render his institutions victorious. "A bruised reed" was not to be broken, the smoking flax was not to be quenched, and neither was his heavenly voice to be "heard in the streets or upon the house tops," to carry his kingdom forward to honor and glory. His mission to earth was one of love, and his design was to subdue the stout heart and stubborn will, by acts of unparalleled kindness.

The meekness and condescension of the Messiah, surpassed that of all others. He entered the haunts of poverty and vice, with remedies from above, and wept with the afflicted sisters at the grave of a deceased brother. That he was a prophet superior to all who had preceded Him, is apparent from his unostentatious predictions in regard to his death, and resurrection,—the destruction of Jerusalem, and the overthrow of the Jewish nation.

Yet He was doomed to the cross, not for his own, but the sins of others.

After laboring thus, night and day, for more than three years, he was betrayed to his enemies by a false friend. In his trial, truth was trampled in the dust—justice was scoffed at—false witnesses swore away his life, and his condemnation was extorted from the governor of Judea. Jesus was condemned to die; he stood alone in mock robes, forsaken and friendless, yet he murmured not. He "came to seek and save the lost," and his own precious blood was to be the price of our redemption. To Calvary, near Jerusalem, his enemies led Him, and while he gazed upon his timid, yet tearful followers, He said: "You daughters of Jerusalem, weep not for Me, but for yourselves and your children; for if they do these things in the green tree, what shall be done in the dry?" He died between two thieves; but the insult to heaven was so monstrous that, the sun vailed himself in night's thick darkness; the rocks were broken about Jerusalem, and the vail of the temple on Zion's hill was rent in twain from top to bottom. Jesus died. His mourning and heart-stricken friends, begged his body of Pilate, and placed it in Joseph's new tomb. A guard of iron-hearted soldiers was placed at the sepulcher, to prevent his disciples from taking away his body, and reporting, as his murderers pretended, that He had risen from the dead, as He had said He would do.

The soldiers stood firm the first and second day, but on the third morning, at God's majesty, they cowardly fell as dead men,—the angel rolled away the stone from the mouth of the sepulcher, but he was not within. The Jews paid the soldiers to report that, while they slept his disciples stole away his body. Such is the absurd and incredible testimony, which must be received, or the world must confess, that God raised his beloved Son from the tomb.

He appeared first to Mary Magdalene in the Garden, then to the eleven, next to "above five hundred who saw him at once," and last of all, to Paul, who was adopted out of due time.

He ate, drank, and conversed with his disciples, who were to be his witnesses to the nations. When He assembled them on the mount of Olives, to deliver his last and great commission for the salvation of sinners, He said: "*All authority in heaven and in earth is given to me, go ye, therefore, teach all nations, baptizing them into the name of the Father, and of the Son, and of the Holy Spirit; teaching them* (*the baptized*) *to observe all things whatsoever I have commanded you, and lo, I am with you always*, (to confirm your word) *even to the conclusion of the age.*"

Mark informs us, that "They went forth, and preached everywhere, the Lord working with them, and confirming the word with signs following."

Such is the Gospel of Christ, written by Matthew, Mark, Luke and John, and all true ministers of the word, have preached and relied upon these facts for the conversion of the world.

The reader will please notice that, the object of the Gospel is to produce faith in them that hear it; and we may add, the effect of this faith of Christ, is to work an entire revolution of the affections and feelings of the soul toward God and man.

"These things are written," said the beloved John, "that ye might believe, that Jesus is the Christ, the Son of God, and that believing ye might have life through his name."

When our object is to convince men of the truth, we are to preach, "Christ and

Him crucified," with the fullest confidence that the means will accomplish the end designed.

SECOND DIVISION OF THE NEW TESTAMENT.

The Book of Conversions.

While the myriads of the honest sons and daughters of earth, old as well as young, in every age from the apostles to the present, would have freely given worlds, had they possessed them, for the plain and infallible treatise on the subject of becoming Christians, owing to the great confusion that has prevailed in reading the Scriptures, few, comparatively, have found it. Such a work, however, God has graciously given to the world, through his Son. This, in our version, is called

"THE ACTS OF THE APOSTLES."

The apostles acting under the commission of our Saviour, preached the Gospel as the Spirit gave them "utterance;" when the people heard with understanding, they turned to God, and by submitting to Jesus Christ in the act of baptism, were constituted heirs of God and joint heirs with our Lord Jesus Christ. It was the province of Luke, the physician, to attend the apostles' administrations of the Gospel, assisting in every needful work, and when aliens became obedient to the faith, he, with the utmost care and impartiality, recorded the facts connected with the conversions, and gave a volume to the world completely adapted to the exigencies of the whole race.

It would be proper, furthermore, to suggest, that this book, also throws much light upon the planting of churches, the appointment of officers, and their general growth in grace and the knowledge of the truth. A few brief details, will not only make the main point plain, but leave its truth beyond dispute.

In the first chapter, Luke rehearses the prominent facts in the ministry of John the Baptist; the ascension of our Lord from Mt. Olivet; the assemblage of the hundred and twenty at Jerusalem, in expectation of the Holy Spirit, and the appointment of Matthias to the place from which Judas, by transgression, fell.

The second chapter opens with the descent of the Holy Spirit in the day of Pentecost, upon the waiting disciples; the astonished condition of the multitude,—their scoffs and wild conjectures in regard to its import; the preaching of the first sermon by Peter, in obedience to the new commission; its convincing and quickening influence on them that heard—their cry, "What shall we do?" the answer of the inspired Peter,—"Repent and be baptized every one of you, in the name of Jesus Christ, for the remission of sins;" their gladly receiving the word, and being baptized; their continuance in the apostles' teaching; in the breaking of bread in prayers, and fellowship after their submission; and, finally, the establishment of the Church and the additions of the saved to it. Unless the student of the Christian religion, should master this chapter, there is little hope of success in the balance of the book. The details relate chiefly to the introduction of a new era in the moral and intellectual world. The Holy Spirit which was to guide the embassadors of the recently crowned

King, was sent down. Peter, to whom the keys for opening the kingdom and new order of worship, stood up in the name of his Master, to give the laws which were to "go forth out of Zion, and the word of the Lord from Jerusalem," and all the conditions of redemption were new. Through him the people heard the voice of Jehovah—were cut to the heart,—convinced by the words of the spirit in their hearts, he commanded them, first, to renounce their evil ways, and be baptized by Christ's authority, in order to the enjoyment of the proffered pardon. They that gladly heard, were obedient, and they thus placed themselves under the administration of the Prince of Peace.

The third chapter is little more than a repetition of the second. The lame man was healed; the people again assembled; Peter preached the Gospel tidings; commanded them to "Repent and be converted, that, their sins might be blotted out, when the times of refreshing shall come from the presence of the Lord." "And the number of men that believed, was about five thousand." The fourth chapter is but the conclusion of the third, with the additional item that, "The multitude of them that believed, were of one heart and one soul," (iv, 32).

In the fifth chapter, is recorded the apostasy of Ananias with his wife Sapphira, and the terrible judgment of the Lord for their disobedience. Still it is said: "Believers were added to the Lord, multitudes both of men and women."

We have also in this chapter the beginning of persecutions against the disciples of the meek and lowly Jesus. The sixth chapter introduces the subject of the division of labor among the servants of God, in the appointment of seven deacons to supply the wants of the needy. "The word of God," steadily, "increased, the number of the disciples multiplied in Jerusalem, and a great company of the priests were obedient to the faith."

In the seventh, we have the address and death of Stephen, the first martyr for Christ.

In the eighth, we have a history of Philip's preaching in Samaria, and "When they believed Philip preaching the things concerning the kingdom of God and the name of Jesus Christ, they were baptized, both men and women," (Acts viii, 12); also the conversion of Simon, the magician, with his apostasy for "*thinking that* the gift of God could be purchased with money;" and the conversion of the Ethiopian noblemen.

The ninth, contains the conversion of Saul of Tarsus; the tenth, that of Cornelius, and the introduction of the Gospel among the Gentiles.

The eleventh, is a repetition of the tenth, in a different form, with the addition of "the disciples being called Christians first in Antioch." In this strain we might continue through the whole twenty-eight chapters, with similar results.

The Gospel was preached—the people believed—and in obedience became Christians; churches were planted, and nourished in sound doctrine, and thus confirmed in the truth. But at every place, persecution raged, and the disciples willingly suffered for the name of the Lord.

Remember, gentle reader, that when you shall have finished this book, nothing more can be found upon the subject of conversion to God; but should you be satisfied with the acknowledged instructions of the Holy Spirit, you will enjoy not only all the light the world possesses on this point, but a sufficiency to make you wise unto the salvation promised in Christ.

Third Division of the New Testament.

The Book of Discipline, Morality, Piety, Purity of Life and Manners.

Placed after the Acts of the Apostles, the reader will please notice twenty-one Epistles, or Christians' letters. Fourteen were written by Paul, one by James, two by Peter, three by John, and one by Jude. Some of these letters were either written to particular churches, some to Christians scattered throughout certain sections of country, or dispersed abroad, and others to individual disciples.

The manner in which they were addressed, shows very clearly for whom they were written. For instance, Paul, in his first letter, writes, "To all that be in Rome, beloved of God, called to be saints: grace to you, and peace from God our Father and the Lord Jesus Christ." Rom. i, 7.

The first Corinthian letter, he commences thus: "Unto the Church of God, which is at Corinth, to them that are sanctified in Christ Jesus, called to be saints, with all that in every place call upon the name of Jesus Christ our Lord, both theirs and ours; Grace be unto you, and peace from God our Father, and from the Lord Jesus Christ."

In the address of the second letter to the Corinthians, he says: "Paul an apostle of Jesus Christ, by the will of God, and Timothy our brother, unto the Church of God, which is at Corinth, with all the saints who are in all Achaia; Grace be to you, and peace from God our Father, and from the Lord Jesus Christ."

From the Hebrew letter, we learn that it is a logical and Scriptural argument to Jewish Christians, setting forth, in a masterly manner, the superiority of the Christian over the Jewish institution, with the evidences of Jehovah's faithfulness to such as honor his appointments. The epistle to Philemon, is addressed by Paul and Timothy "to Philemon, Apphia, Archippus, and the Church in his house. Grace to you and peace from God our Father, and the Lord Jesus Christ." These will serve as illustrations of all Paul's letters.

James wrote to the Christians of the "Twelve tribes, scattered abroad." Peter wrote to the "Elect strangers, scattered throughout Pontus, Gallatia, Cappadocia, Asia, and Bithynia." John, in his first epistle, wrote "to little children" in the Lord, "'because' their sins were forgiven for his name's sake;" "'to fathers,' because they had known him from the beginning," and "to young men, because" they were "strong and had overcome the wicked one." 1 John ii, 12–14.

His second, was addressed to an "Elect lady, whom he loved in the truth," and the third was affectionately inscribed, "unto the well beloved Gaius."

Jude wrote "To them that are sanctified by God the Father, and preserved in Jesus Christ and called."

These addresses afford ample information in regard to the character of the persons who were to be profited by the various letters in the New Testament, and that they were essential to perfect the system of our Lord, must appear from the subjects discussed, and the manner in which the different points were handled.

All those addressed in these twenty-one epistles, were called justified, sanctified and saved; and it was the object of the writers to free them from the dangerous tendencies of existing errors; and, to direct the mind in all the practical principles of the religion of Jesus Christ. In these letters, we find the only perfect and infallible system of Church government on earth. The various duties of teachers and the taught, are discussed with equal perspicuity; and there is not a single offense against good morals and purity of life, in reference to which, we have not complete instruction.

The subject of *temperance* is elaborately treated in all its bearings, and all the temperance associations of the world, must fall far short of equaling the institutes of temperance in the New Testament. The covet ous man and extortioner, have their place definitely assigned to them. The adulterer, fornicator, the unclean, and lascivious, the idolater, wizard, man of tricks,—the man of hatred, wrath or strife in his heart, the murderer, drunkard, reviler, and factionist, are pointed downward to death and misery.

Christians are instructed in every grace. Hence we hear the apostle exhorting the brethren to, "Add to their faith courage, knowledge, temperance, patience, godliness, brotherly kindness and charity, or universal love," with the promise that, "they who do these things, shall never fall; for so an abundant enterance shall be administered unto you, into the everlasting kingdom of our Lord and Saviour Jesus Christ." 2 Peter i, 5–11.

In few words, these letters constitute not only the discipline of the Church, in a general sense, but they afford so ample instruction, to husband and wife, parent and child, master and servant, youth and senior, married and unmarried, widows and maidens, rich and poor, Jew and Greek, male and female, that nothing is needed to perfect character. If, therefore, we desire rules for church government, we have them in our Third division of the New Testament. If we need a book on conversation, courtesy, politeness, good manners, Paul and John are as far superior to Lord Chesterfield and Count D'Orsay, as heaven is superior to earth. As the instructions afforded, make the true gentlemen, or lady, in the highest, and only Christian sense, it would be by no means light or irreverent, to style the division, by way of eminence, God's Book of Purity and Good Manners. Let these inspired letters, oh reader! be your constant companions through life.

Fourth Division of the New Testament.

The Book of Revolutions.

We very respectfully ask the reader to entertain no prejudice against our novel, "title page." A little examination and careful reflection will show the propriety of the style. The title in king James's version is:

"THE REVELATION OF ST. JOHN THE DIVINE."

This smacks very plainly of a dark age, yet an age more recent than the apostolic, and of Rome, the inventress of foreign titles for the servants of God. Worse still, the title, "Revelation of St. John," is in fact, not true. It contradicts the very first verse in the revelation itself. The verse reads, "The Revelation of Jesus Christ, which God gave unto him, to show unto his servants things which must shortly come to pass, and He sent and signified it by his angel unto his servant John."

From these palpable declarations, it is evident that our title, though novel, cannot be worse than the one we have, it may be better — entirely appropriate. As names were originally significant, and when wisely used, may still be so, the essence of this last division of the Bible, will suggest most readily the style of the work.

While John, the apostle and "beloved disciple," was in banishment on the lonely island of Patmos in the Ægean sea, "For the word of God and for the testimony of Jesus Christ," he says: "I was in the spirit on the Lord's day, and heard behind me a great voice, as of a trumpet; saying, I am Alpha and Omega, the first and the last: and, what thou seest, write in a book, and send it unto the seven churches which are in Asia." Rev. i, 10, 11. It will be kept in mind that, this book was to be sent to the seven churches in Asia, and in the special addresses to respective churches, we have the future history, not only of these churches, but also of the Christian and anti-christian world boldly shadowed forth. The apostasy, from the simplicity of the Gospel of Christ, is represented under the figure of a proud woman, seated upon broad waters, and upon her forehead was a name written, "MYSTERY, BABYLON THE GREAT, THE MOTHER OF HARLOTS AND ABOMINATIONS OF THE EARTH." The true church is represented by "A woman clothed with the sun and the moon under her feet, and upon her head a crown of twelve stars. And the woman fled into the wilderness, where she hath a place prepared of God, that they should feed her there, a thousand two hundred and threescore days." Rev. xii, 1–6. This woman had the promise of strength and protection from God, and her children were to overcome by the blood of the Lamb and the word of the Lord." The opposing woman was finally to be destroyed, with all her children. She is described also as a city which had made "all nations drunk with the wine of the wrath of her fornication." And John says: "I heard another voice from heaven, saying, Come out of her, my people, that ye be not partakers of her sins, and that ye receive not of her plagues." Rev. xviii, 4.

We wish to say to the reader that, we doubt not that this is a representation of the Romish hierarchy, with her numerous daughters, or sectarian institutions, built upon forms and creeds taken from the mother, all of which are to greater or less extent, opposed to the true Christian institution. The sin and destruction of this, "Mother of abominations, are thus described. Her sins have reached unto heaven, and God hath remembered her iniquities

Reward her even as she rewarded you, and double unto her double according to her works, in the cup which she hath filled, fill to her double. Her plagues shall come in one day, death, and mourning, and famine; and she shall be utterly burned with fire; for strong is the Lord God, who judgeth her. Rev. xviii, 4–8. Again: "They cast dust on their heads, and cried, weeping, wailing, and saying, alas, alas, that great city, wherein were made rich, all that had ships in the sea by reason of her costliness; for in one hour, is she made desolate."

"Rejoice over her thou heaven, and ye holy apostles, and prophets; for God hath avenged you on her. And a mighty angel took up a stone, like a great millstone, and cast it into the sea, saying, thus with violence shall that great city Babylon be thrown down, and shall be found no more at all." Rev. xviii, 19–21.

The last and grandest revolution in this drama of earth, is recorded in the conclusion of the twentieth chapter.

"And I saw the dead, small and great stand before God; and the books were opened; and another book was opened, which is the book of life: and the dead were judged out of these things written in the books according to their works. And the sea gave up the dead which were in it, and death and hell, (the grave and the unseen world) delivered up the dead which were in them; and they were judged every man according to his works. And death and hell were cast into the lake of fire. This is the second death. And whosoever was not found written in the book of life, was cast into the lake of fire."

Now, reader, might we not correctly style this "the Book of Revolutions?" The probability, in addition to the revolutions that have taken place in religion for nearly eighteen hundred years, and such as are yet to occur, is that most of the great national struggles from the birth of Christianity to the conclusion of this wonderful age, are more or less vividly portrayed in this vast picture-book of the universe.

When we read it, therefore, as the only book of imagery in the New Testament, we will most likely possess ourselves of the great thoughts therein contained.

Concluding Remarks.

While we look upon the surface of religious society, the strife, disorder, and general opposition, seem to say, "Professed Christians will never be united, and the world will not believe that the Father sent the Son to be a Saviour;" but upon closer examination, we are constrained to admit, that godly men everywhere, speak and practice the same things. Could the world be induced to study the sacred Scriptures, upon the proper plan, we see no reason why all the pious should not rejoice in the same great cardinal principles of the Christian institution.

To the youth, who may read this little work, we would very respectfully suggest the propriety, not only of reading according to the rules and divisions we have submitted, but also of appropriating a part of every day to this work.

One hour in twenty-four, given to the study of the Bible for a single year, would tell mightily in the religious intelligence of the individual, or of the society that will adopt and pursue this plan.

To teachers of religion, we would urge the necessity of directing their thoughts and energies, to means and modes to induce those under their influence, to study the Scriptures systematically. Fine sermons can be of no service, if the people learn not the truth; and finally, we give it as our most solemn conviction, that all religious efforts, in which the careful study of the word of God is neglected, must prove abortive. We conclude with the very expressive words of the "beloved" John. "Blessed is he that readeth, and they that hear the words of this prophecy, and keep those things which are written therein: for the time is at hand."

THE END.

BOOKS AND STATIONERY.

The Evidences of Christianity—A Debate between Robert Owen, of New Lanark, Scotland, and Alexander Campbell, President of Bethany College, Va.; containing an examination of the "Social System," and all the systems of Skepticism of ancient and modern times; 5th Edition. $1 50

The Biography of Elder Barton W. Stone—Written by himself; with additions and reflections, by Elder John Rogers.................. 75

Predestination, and the Foreknowledge of God—A debate between Rev. James Matthews, Pastor of the Presbyterian church, Carlisle, Ky., and Elder Benjamin Franklin, pastor of Clinton St. Christian Church, Cincinnati............... 1 00

The Christian Primer—For the use of Sunday Schools and Families. Per dozen............ 75

Scripture Questions and Answers—For little Children. Per dozen 60

Macaulay's History of England, 2 volumes in one.. 1 25

Christian Hymn Book—sheep.............. 40
" " " —roan.............. 50
" " " —turkey gilt......... 1 00
" " " —extra " 1 25
" " " —velvet and gold..... 5 00

The Christian Psalmist—A collection of Tunes and Hymns for the use of worshiping Assemblies, Singing and Sunday Schools, by S. W. Leonard & A. D. Fillmore.................... 75

The Responsibility of the Disciples of Christ as Stewards of God—By Elder P. S. Fall. Per 100.............................. 2 50

Temperance Address—A simple, infallible rule of right moral action, deduced from the Word of God and right reason, and applicable to the pursuits of life. By elder John Rogers. Per dozen 50

Bible Questions — Designed to aid Sunday Schools and Families in the study of Man's only Guide to a happy immortality. By L. L. Pinkerton.

The Universal Musician—A new Collection of Secular and Sacred Music, designed for Schools, Musical Associations, and Social Music parties; with a new and comprehensive plan of instruction, embracing the various systems of Notation; by A. D. Fillmore........................... 75

The Complete Works of Josephus, with Explanatory Notes and observations: plain....... 1 00
Ditto, gilt......... 1 10
Ditto, embossed... 1 25

Scenes and Legends........................ 1 00

Course of Creation.......................... 1 25

Romanism not Christianity................. 1 00

Rice and Blanchard on Slavery............ 1 25

Philosophy of the Plan of Salvation....... 75

Mississippi Valley.......................... 1 00

Three Great Temptations.................. 1 00

Life of Chalmers............................ 1 25

Vegetable World............................ 1 25

University Sermons......................... 1 00

Proverbs for the People.................... 85

History Baptist Missions.................... 1 25

Scenes in Old Dominion.................... 1 00
Church in Earnest.......................... 50
Earnest Ministry........................... 1 00
Man. Primeval............................. 1 25
Annual Scientific Discovery................ 1 25
Pascal's Thoughts.......................... 1 00
Classical Studies, by Edwards............... 85
The Great Teacher.......................... 75
The Great Commission...................... 1 00
Harris's Missionary Sermons................ 75
Foster on Missions......................... 50
Foster's Life and Thoughts.................. 40
Memoir of Bennett.......................... 85
Montaign's Endless Study................... 1 25
Fuller and Wayland on Slavery.............. 65
Person and Work of Christ.................. 50
Baptist Psalmist........................... 1 00
Jerusalem Mission—Under the direction of the American Christian Missionary Society, compiled by D. S. Burnet. Price 75 cents, or twenty copies.................................... 10 00
The Rum Plague...................... 35 cents.
Temperance Musician.................. 25 "
Rogers on Temperance, per dozen.......... $1 00
Barnes' Notes.
Clarke's Commentaries.
Comprehensive Commentary.
Burket on New Testament.
McKnight on Epistles.

JUVENILE BOOKS.

Natural History of Quadrupeds.

Natural History of Land Birds.

" " " Water Birds.

Customs of America.

Customs of Europe.

Juvenile Sports and Amusements.

Book of Heroes.

Stories from Roman History.

" " Grecian History.

Scripture Biography from Adam to David— 7 volumes.

Child at Home.

Elijah the Tishbite.

Bible Stories.

History of Jonah.

" " Josiah.

Youth's Book of Natural Theology.

Ripley's Notes.

Budge's Exposition of Proverbs.

Anderson's Annals of the English Bible.

Union Bible Dictionary, etc., etc.

☞ Any other Theological Books will be furnished at the shortest notice, and the lowest prices, for cash.

The Principles and Objects of the Religious Reformation, urged by A. Campbell and others, by R. Richardson, Professor in Bethany College. Price from 20 cents to 75 cents, according to the binding.

ENCYCLOPEDIA of Religious Knowledge; or, Dictionary of the Bible, Theology, Religious Biography, all Religious Ecclesiastical History and Missions; Definitions of all Religious Terms, and an impartial account of the Principal Christian Denominations, etc., etc., containing 1275 double column royal octavo pages, beautifully and substantially bound in gilt calf. Price only.............. $5 00

Eclectic Series of School Books, just received and for sale, wholesale and retail, at the CHRISTIAN BOOKSTORE.

McGuffey's Readers and Spellers.

Ray's Arithmetic, and Algebra.

Pinneo's Grammar.

Hemans' Young Ladies' Reader.

SUNDAY SCHOOL LIST.

Books and other publications suitable for Sunday School and Family Instruction.

Bibles, 40 cents each and upward.

Testaments, 8 cents each and upward.

Scripture Questions and Answers, by B. F. Hall, paper covers, per dozen, 40 cents.

Primers, Spellers, and Readers, at various prices.

Alphabets on Cards, 2 sizes, 3 and 4 cents each.

Reward Tickets, with passage from New Testament on each, per 1000, 50 cents.

Picture Reward Tickets, with passage and a Hymn, per 100, 25 cents.

Small Illustrated Books, paper cover, done up in neat packages, containing fifteen different books, well calculated to instruct very young readers, per package, 15 cents.

Books beautifully Illustrated, suitable for Rewards; bound in muslin, 15 cents each and upward.

Maps—Map of Palestine, 14 by 22 inches, on sheets, each,.... ....$0 20

Map of Palestine, by S. P. Durbin. This Map is drawn on muslin, is five feet in length, each...$1 25

Map of Apostle Paul's Travels; on muslin, 7 feet by 4, lines bold and strong, to be seen by a whole school at one view, each.................... $2 50

Map of the Journeyings of the Children of Israel, by J. P. Durbin, on cloth, five feet by four, each.................................... $2 00

Teachers' Class Book, arranged for keeping names of scholars, noting their attendance, and listing, weekly, the library book given to each. This is a very useful little book; each, 8 cents.

Superintendents' Roll-Book, with directions for its use.......................................$0 15

The Beautifully Illustrated Sunday School Library, selected by the Publishing Committee of the Board. It consists of 60 Volumes, and is furnished for.................................. $10 00

Sunday School Hymn Book: cloth, per dozen 1 25
" " " " paper, " " 75

The Sunday School Journal, now in the 3d volume, will be found a valuable aid in interesting children in the Sunday School. It is now issued twice a month. It is desirable that all subscriptions commence with the volume, which begins in may. Back numbers on hand. TERMS—Single copy, a year, always in advance, 35 cents; four copies, to one address, $1 ; twenty, $5; fifty, $10.

Every variety of Stationery; writing papers of all sizes and qualities in any quantity. Pens of every description, pencils, pencil-points, rubbers, rulers and other appointments for the writing-table.

Ministers of the Gospel, are furnished with *our* publications *one third off,* for cash, and they will find it to the advantage of their flocks and of themselves to circulate our works. All other books will be put at the Lowest Rates Possible.

The Board of Publication pledge themselves that all cash orders sent addressed AMERICAN CHRISTIAN PUBLICATION SOCIETY, *corner of Eighth and Walnut Streets, Cincinnati, Ohio,* will be attended to promptly; the Board having secured the services of Agents exclusively devoted to the business of the Society.

Through their Agents, they are also prepared to fill all orders for any Books to be had West or East. Receive and attend to any orders for Printing, Publishing, and Binding Books, Pamphlets, Periodicals, and Minutes, etc., on fair terms. In ordering, be particular to send the cash and address.

Organ of the Society, "CHRISTIAN AGE."

www.ingramcontent.com/pod-product-compliance
Lightning Source LLC
LaVergne TN
LVHW021415110826
845150LV00007B/1929

* 9 7 8 1 4 2 5 5 1 1 0 6 7 *